W9-ATH-234

The Secular Promise

MARTIN JARRETT-KERR

The Secular Promise

›››◊‹‹‹

Christian Presence Amid
Contemporary Humanism

Introduction by
M. A. C. WARREN

FORTRESS PRESS
PHILADELPHIA

IN MEMORIAM

Harold Evelyn Hubbard

Bishop

ob. 23 May 1953

PRINTED IN GREAT BRITAIN

General Introduction

›››◆‹‹‹

CHRISTIANS are being presented by the contemporary world with what is, in many ways, a unique opportunity of demonstrating the Gospel. Scarcely less unique is the opportunity being offered to them of discovering in a new and deeper way what the Gospel is. Those are large claims. Can they be justified?

What is this unique opportunity? At the very least it is the opportunity presented to Christians to demonstrate the fundamental truth of the Gospel that it is a universal message, whose relevance is not limited to any one culture, to any one system of thought, to any one pattern of activity. That is by no means the truism that it may appear to be. For more than four centuries the expansion of the Christian Church has coincided with the economic, political, and cultural expansion of Western Europe. Viewed from the standpoint of the peoples of Asia, and to a growing extent from that of the peoples of Africa, this expansion has been an aggressive attack on their own way of life. Quite inevitably the Christian Faith has for many in these lands been inextricably bound up with this Western aggression. But it has also to be admitted quite frankly that during these centuries the missionaries of the Christian Church have commonly assumed that

Western civilization and Christianity were two aspects of the same gift which they were commissioned to offer to the rest of mankind.

This assumption was sometimes quite conscious and was explicitly stated. More often it was quite unconscious and would have been indignantly denied. But in neither case are we called upon to judge our fathers. Their sincerity can hardly be disputed. Their self-sacrificing devotion finds its monument today in the world-wide diffusion of the Christian Faith, the existence, in almost every country of the world, of a community of Christians recognizably part of the Universal Church.

What we are called upon to recognize is that in the world of our time there is a widespread revolt against any form of domination by the West. Nations whose political independence was only achieved 'yesterday' or is only about to be achieved 'tomorrow' can be excused for having their own interpretation of the past, an interpretation unlikely to coincide with that which is prevalent in the West. This very waning of Western influence is in part our Christian opportunity. We are freer today than we have ever been to serve the Gospel without the risk of confusion between that Gospel and the 'power' of the West.

But that is not all. The peoples of Asia and Africa, in their revolt against domination by the West, are presenting a specific challenge to the Christian Faith. In what does this consist?

There are three main ingredients in this challenge. *First*, there is a critical evaluation of the Christian religion which rejects it as something inherently Western, as something which fails to correspond to the *felt* needs of Asia and Africa. Christianity is, in such judgement, altogether too Western in its character and in the form which it assumes in its local manifestations. This rejection is the more serious in that Asian and African peoples are themselves, like us in the West, confronted by the bewildering demands of the modern world. All the old landmarks are disappearing. Everywhere there is a desperate search for some inner basis of security, some inner assurance which can enable men and women to face the storm. In the sequel, particularly in Asia, but not only there, the peoples of these countries are seeking to find this psychic security by digging deep into their own past. This is at once an expression of their revolt against the West and one explanation of the renaissance of the great ethnic religions. Further to this it is to be noted that in a new way these ancient religions are becoming themselves missionary. No longer content to be on the defensive, they are offering themselves as answers to the questionings of mankind.

Here is a situation which is new. Only once before, and then in its earliest centuries, has the Christian Church had to face a comparable challenge to its claim to meet the deepest needs of man's heart and mind. The devotees of Mithras, the mystery cults of the Mediterranean world, the Gnostics in that earlier day were serious competitors with the message of the Gospel. Their appeal failed. There followed the long thousand years during which Europe was isolated from the rest of mankind and built for itself its own peculiar civilization. Then suddenly, drawing on its inner dynamism, a dynamism closely related to its faith, the European world overflowed its narrow boundaries and began its great expansion. For a time it appeared as if nothing could arrest this expansion. It is of some importance to recognize that it is by no means certain that anything can! The scientific view of the world, with all its implications about human survival, is Western in origin. Communism and nationalism are Western concepts. It may well be doubted if anything can arrest the advance of all mankind towards something like a common civilization – if common destruction is avoided. Nevertheless there is, at the moment, a significant pause in the impetus of Western expansion in its Christian expression. The challenge to Christians is precisely this that the ethnic religions as well as secularist philosophies of life are offering themselves as the basis of the new world civilization. Both deny the relevance of Christianity.

The *second* challenge follows from the first. Can the Christian Faith not only prove its ability to meet the deep human needs of our time but also make peoples of different cultural backgrounds feel at home in the new world? This is a more complex task than would appear. For it is part of our paradoxical situation that, at a moment when the world is becoming so obviously interdependent, every nation in it is seeking to assert its own independence. And religion and culture are the means by which independence is asserted. Has the Christian Church got a Gospel to meet this situation? We may put the question this way – can the Christians of the West accept the fact that the expression which Christianity will receive in its Asian and African forms may well be, almost certainly will be, in many respects very different indeed from what we know in the West? That again could be worded as follows – are we of the West prepared to trust the Holy Spirit to lead the Christians of Asia and Africa, or must a controlling Western hand be permanently resting on the Ark of God? Let no one imagine that those questions will find an easy or unanimous response from Western Christians.

There remains a *third* challenge. The Christian Church has not yet seriously faced the theological problem of 'co-existence' with other religions. The very term seems to imply the acceptance of some limitation of the universal relevance of the Gospel. Can that be accepted? It can hardly be doubted that the answer must be 'no'. Are we then shut up to the alternatives of what in some disguise or other must be an aggressive attack on the deeply held convictions of those who live by other Faiths than our own?

This book, originally one in the *Christian Presence Series*, has been designed to express a deliberate recognition of the challenge outlined above and to suggest that there is a way in which they can be met without any betrayal of the Gospel – indeed in deeper loyalty to that Gospel's real content.

First of the demands presented to us by this understanding of the contemporary world is a *glad* acceptance of the new situation in which the Christian Faith can everywhere be distinguished from its past historical association with Western political, economic and cultural aggression. Here is the 'great new fact of our time', every whit as great a fact as the existence of the Church in every land. Here is our great new opportunity, even though it may well be an opportunity to witness through suffering. The Cross, after all, was not a symbol of imperial domination but of the *imperium* of sacrifice. The Christian Faith has nothing to lose by suffering. In and through suffering it can perhaps speak home to the hearts and minds of suffering mankind better than in any other way.

Second of the demands upon us, to march with our gladness, is a deep humility, by which we remember that God has not left himself without witness in any nation at any time. When we approach the man of another faith than our own it will be in a spirit of expectancy to find how God has been speaking to him and what new understanding of the grace and love of God we may ourselves discover in this encounter.

Our first task in approaching another people, another culture, another religion is to take off our shoes, for the place we are approaching is holy. Else we may find ourselves treading on men's dreams. More serious still, we may forget that God was here before our arrival. We have, then, to ask what is the authentic religious content in the experience of the Muslim, the Hindu, the Buddhist, or whoever he may be. We may, if we have asked humbly and respectfully, still reach the conclusion that our brothers have started from a false premise and reached a faulty conclusion. But we must not arrive at our judgement from outside their religious situation. We have to try to sit where they sit, to enter sympathetically into the pains and griefs and joys of their history and see how those pains and griefs and joys have determined the premises of their argument. We have, in a word, to be 'present' with them.

The present volume represents an attempt to explore the religion of Western man in what, in the West, can with some degree of accuracy be described as the post-Christian Age. Of course that term begs many questions. Were the ages of faith really Christian? Might not the seventeenth century in which men fought so fiercely over religion be even more entitled to be called an age of faith than the Middle Ages themselves? Did not the conscience of man in the West arrive at a higher degree of sensitivity in the nineteenth century than ever before? Is that conscience not becoming even more sensitive today? Such questions may well challenge us to examine the phrase 'post-Christian age'.

Yet it can hardly be disputed that we live at a time when, for a vast proportion of Western mankind, anything which cannot be conceived in terms of Man and his world, as that is being explored by the natural sciences, is dismissed as being not 'real', and therefore as being without interest. In such a climate of thought the arts find themselves on the defensive. Indeed man himself is more and more on the defensive. To the question 'who am I?' there is no clear answer. Contemporary humanism in all its multiple forms is, in one sense, a comprehensive attempt to define Man, to give Man meaning. And this attempt is as truly religious in its significance for man as are the attempts of the great religions to arrive at different kinds of answers.

For the Christian, therefore, it is necessary to ask where in the ferment of contemporary humanism can be discerned the operation of the Holy Spirit of Wisdom. For this ferment is all part of that common human experience of an expanding Universe of Knowledge by which we are being led into new truth. Unless we are to think of the Holy Spirit as having abdicated we are, as Christians, bound to ask what he is doing in our world. And, as Christians, we should be no less sure that this enquiry will produce results.

In this volume Fr Martin Jarrett-Kerr, of the Community of the Resurrection, draws upon wide reading to show the inwardness of much contemporary humanism, to illustrate the proper nature of its challenge to the Christian mind, and to indicate how within a movement of thought which at times seems to be so profoundly anti-religious there is nevertheless to be found evidence of the *anima naturaliter Christiana*. It is because our author, having explored widely, has found the Christian presence in contemporary humanism that he can with such confidence give this volume the title of *The Secular Promise*.

Furthermore it is of some importance to recognize that this volume has a peculiar right to find a place in a series which deals with the Christian presence among the ancient religions of mankind, for to an ever increasing extent these religions, like Christianity itself, are all finding themselves involved in contemporary humanism. As a recent writer has said, speaking of Christianity –

> Modern man is not 'out there' to be spoken to; he is within the being of every Christian trying to understand.

No less is this true of the men of other Faiths. Fr Jarrett-Kerr here adds a new dimension to our understanding of the Christian Presence in man's religious consciousness.

M. A. C. WARREN

Contents

Acknowledgments

I am grateful to Canon M. A. C. Warren for his constant encouragement and valuable criticism; to the Church Union Summer School of Sociology, which over the years has taught me to think constantly about the relation of theology to society – I could wish that I had learned my lessons better; to the Librarians of the Cardiff City and Kensington Central Libraries, for help with books and references; and last, but not least, to Miss P. Greatbatch for painstaking work on the index.

Acknowledgments are given to the following for permission to use copyright material: The Rationalist Press (*Rationalist Annual* 1961), Dr H. J. Muller (contribution to *The Humanist Frame*), Ed. du Seuil (L. S. Senghor, *Pierre Teilhard de Chardin et la politique africaine*), Grasset (I. Lepp, *Psychoanalyse de l'athéisme moderne*), Allen & Unwin (K. M. Pannikar, *The Foundations of a New India*), Free Press of Glencoe (M. Argyle, *Religious Behaviour*), Gollancz (E. E. Hirschmann, *On Human Unity*), Harper & Row (G. Lukacs, *The Meaning of Contemporary Realism*, T. S. Szasz, *The Myth of Mental Illness*), Harvard Univ. Press (A. C. Crombie, *Augustine to Galileo*), Humanities Press (P. Winch, *The Idea of a Social Science*), Kings Crown Press (Wen-Han Kiang, *The Chinese Student Movement*), Knopf (A. Camus, *The Rebel* [*L'Homme Révolté*]), Atlantic-Little, Brown & Co. (E. Heller, *The Ironic German*), Macmillan (A. Koestler, *The Sleepwalkers*), Roy Publ. (W. Mellers, *Music and Society*), St Martin's Press (A. Macbeath, *Experiments in Living*), Viking Press (P. Rieff, *Freud: The Mind of the Moralist*), Wesleyan Univ. Press (N. O. Brown, *Life Against Death*).

Preface

›››◊‹‹‹

THIS is intended to be a work of Christian exploration, not of Christian apologetics. The apologist is concerned to defend the Faith against unbelief or false belief. He tends therefore to watch for chances to trip up the adversary. The danger is that this makes him both judge and prosecuting counsel; the late Professor John Laird defined apologetics as a game in which the goal-keeper is also the referee.

I am concerned to discover the strength and weakness of modern secularism, its inner contradictions but also its power of self-criticism and recuperation: and to see whether there may not be a 'presence of Christ' amid all this.

This, however, raises an obvious problem. Many explanatory volumes such as this have tried to detect a 'presence' of Christ in non-Christian religions – Buddhism, Hinduism, Islam and the rest. Their task was not easy: for there are many different versions of some of these religions. Nevertheless, ten people describing (say) Buddhism, though they might give very different descriptions, would all produce accounts which would be recognizably about the same religion. But twenty different accounts of 'secularism' today might each appear to be about a different topic.

This must be the excuse for the fact that this book is so full of quotations. It is not merely that I do not want to play the game of setting up a target of my own devising and then riddling it; I want also to provide enough material to make the phenomenon 'secularism' recognizable. Of course, the selection has been subjective; but I have done my best. At least I can claim that ninety per cent of the writers I have quoted are 'secular' thinkers.

Indeed, it is likely that I shall give the impression of having blessed a great many features of contemporary life and society which other Christians may feel should not be blessed. There are certainly those who believe that the Christian forces should present a firmer and more uncompromising face to 'the world'. In one sense I believe they are right; but unfortunately wherever I see them doing so, I think that they do it badly, that they try to batter down the wrong walls, and do not always understand the nature of their own power. So this book is above all a plea for understanding.

Naturally, I believe that a Christian humanism is in fact the right goal. But Christians are no more exempt than secular humanists from the error of mistaking a temporary halt for the terminus. So if I seem to have condoned a secularism that gives the impression of being self-sufficient, it has been precisely because I have tried to keep at the back of my mind St Paul's awareness that

> *We* are not sufficient of ourselves to think anything as of our selves; but our sufficiency is of God.

MARTIN JARRETT-KERR, C.R.

1

The Anatomy of Secularism

›››◇‹‹‹

IT is one of the minor paradoxes of contemporary Western society that precisely the towns least well equipped to accommodate modern traffic are among those most popular among motorists. A nostalgia for the old and the quaint ensures that the narrowest of streets receive the largest number of vehicles. One suspects that part of the nostalgia is for a religio-centric culture, clustered visibly round a church building. We should not like today to live in such a culture, perhaps; but it is a nice complex to contemplate, even to admire. It is still possible, motoring through country areas in Great Britain – or in the Middle West of the United States – to picture, from what one sees architecturally demonstrated, a society of which the Church is the warm, magnetic centre. (No doubt the relation of mosque to dwellings in Muslim towns suggests a similar, visible, theocentrism.) The romantic image of a Church-centred community may well distort the reality – a reality of bigotry, inward-looking stagnation and sometimes ecclesiastical oppression, from which Western man can be grateful for having been delivered. But even a suitably corrected image still has power to intrigue, if not to attract us.

This is confirmed by one of the few conclusions of 'religious sociology' which seems to have been fairly widely and with some degree of probability established by statistical comparisons: the correlation between size of urban 'complex' and religious attachment. A survey of weekly church attendance in Great Britain gave the following figures:

Town under 10,000	10,000-100,000	100,000-1 m	over 1 m
17%	15%	15%	12%

This compares interestingly with figures obtained on slightly different, but parallel, criteria in the United States:

(The reference is to 'Membership' of Christian churches, and the figures are not the percentage of the population but the ratio of the actual/expected number of members. That is why the indices are low):

Farms	under 2,500	2,500-10,000	10,000-100,000	100,000-500,000	over 500,000
6·8%	5·83%	5·54%	4·86%	3·98%	3·34%

The almost exact similarity of the downward graph is sufficiently striking to suggest that there must be a fairly clear correspondence between the factors.[1] If so, then the growth in number and size of large cities in Western Europe and the United States is likely to have had something to do with the spread of 'secularism'. London in 1800 had 959,310 inhabitants; by 1850 it had over 2 million. Paris had 500,000 in 1800, and over 1 million by 1850. By the year 1900 there were 11

[1] These figures are given in M. Argyle, *Religious Behaviour* (Routledge, 1958), pp. 135-6.

metropolises with more than 1 million inhabitants; by 1930 there were 27 such.[1]

One professional sociologist has made an interesting suggestion, as a result of enquiries he made in South Wales. He first noticed that when the effects of industrial growth upon social mobility and upon the fortunes of the community were studied, there seemed to be a correlation between attendance at public worship and 'associational activities outside industry itself' – active membership of various spare-time organizations. It seems, from the industrial areas he studied, that where the community is expanding (in numbers, and in standards of life), participation in public worship *and* in 'associated life' decline. And then he goes on to suggest that there may have been a connection between 'working class' links with institutional religion, surviving almost up till the present day, in certain Welsh mining valleys, and the Welsh traditional industries, which were of a type that allowed a high level of autonomy to the individual worker. (This, he says, was particularly so with the hand-mill, but also with the mining industry until the mechanized 'longwall' mining methods superseded the older methods, e.g. the 'butty' system.)[2] If there is any truth in this – and studies of Durham mining towns yield somewhat similar evidence – it looks as if there is some connection between 'secularization' and, not merely 'bigness' but impersonality and remoteness

[1] Lewis Mumford, *The Culture of Cities* (Secker, 1938), p. 225.

[2] Unpublished paper: George F. Thomason, 'The Place of the Church in Industry' (cyclostyled copy from Dept. of Industrial Relations, University College, Cardiff).

of responsibility. This is perhaps very obvious. But it has usually been stated in a vague and unverifiable way by the 'intuitionist' school of cultural historians, or by theologically-minded social observers with an anti-Pelagian axe to grind. It comes more respectably from a trained social scientist.

The degrees of secularization, however, differ not only between one city and another, one employment, standard of life, class, etc., and another; but also between one country and another in the West. In a recent international conference held in Europe, to study and evaluate the different understandings of 'secularization', the picture given by the delegates (for what it was worth) of the situation in their various countries was, summarized, as follows:

In *Britain*, welfare institutions are almost entirely secularized, but educational institutions only partially so; the state is secularized in fact but not in appearance; in the universities, the natural sciences – and increasingly, the social sciences – are freeing themselves from metaphysical as well as from religious control . . .; but social life as a whole, public opinion on many controversial topics, and ethical standards generally are still dominated by Christian or quasi-Christian ideas.

France was generally agreed to be the most secularized country in Europe, but Christian thinking and the Christian tradition still have a widespread indirect influence; indeed, it should still be thought of as a Christian country. The schools and the universities are fully secularized as institutions, but professors and teachers hold a wide variety of views ranging from definite Christian to outspoken anti-Christian. The working classes . . . are totally de-Christianized (it is not enough to say they are secularized). Although the cities are more secularized than the villages, the difference is fast disappearing. Among intellectuals, one can find a deep interest in the question of God, combined with a detestation of the Church as an institution historically allied with the state and with the rich . . . .

In *Holland*, scientists have recently more and more been raising theological questions, though they are not influenced by the traditional thinking of the Church. Heated debates are going on among professors. It is still true that 'every Dutchman is a theologian, whether he is a Christian or not'.

West Germany is less religious than Great Britain and less de-Christianized than France. There is a reaction against any claims for power on behalf of the institutionalized Church (e.g., the religious broadcast series, 'Criticisms of the Church', got more positive reaction from the public than any other series). On the other hand, Christian opinion is listened to and discussed when it is relevant and when the power of the Church as an institution is not seen behind it (e.g. 'The Memorandum of the Eight', a document by leading Christians treating of political and social questions, was more discussed by the public than any other statement, Christian or non-Christian). Apparently Christians are still expected to be free to think creatively and to have an impartial concern for people.

In *Portugal* as in *Spain*, Church and state are still intermixed, as in the Middle Ages. Bishops are appointed by the state. The situation in the universities is, however, changing. Many students are Catholic in name but atheist in fact, though they cannot free themselves fully from the medieval concept of Church and state.

In spite of appearance, *Sweden* is more secularized than any other European country except France. Welfare and education, even the theological faculties of universities, are in principle secular. The only thing that has not been secularized is the Established Church! Public debate is dominated by anti-Christian cultural radicals. Most people, however, would consider themselves Christians, though they would resist active participation in church life. There is no Christian party, but Christians involved in different political parties talk about their task to maintain Christian values in society. Scientists have a purely secular approach to their work, but often have a personal interest in religious matters, especially mysticism. Swedish literature is more concerned with religious questions than ever before. It seems as though secularization has advanced so far that people once again feel free to raise religious issues.

In *Finland*, the Church is expected by those outside as well as those within to concentrate on 'religious' activities: preaching the Word of God, burying the dead, etc. It is immediately criticized when it goes beyond this task. Of the Eastern-European countries, *Hungary*, *Bulgaria* and *Rumania* are on the whole still Christian countries in the traditional sense.

In the *Soviet Union*, secularization has progressed much further, but those in contact with the Church still have a medieval conception.

In *Czechoslovakia*, Bohemia is more secularized than Moravia, and Moravia more so than Slovakia. The working classes have almost completely lost contact with the Church, but the vacuum has been filled by the Marxist vision of the meaning of life.

In the *German Democratic Republic*, the degree of secularization which had taken place before the war became visible after 1945. Economics and the concept of social justice are still dominated by the 'metaphysical' ideology of Marxism; in recent years a certain liberation has, however, taken place among scientists. In this historical situation, the task of the Church is to help Marxists become more secularized and less 'metaphysical'.[1]

[1] From an account of the 'Life and Mission of the Church' con-

This conference did not cover other parts of the world, though one delegate spoke of secularization in India. But no doubt similar comparative pictures could be given of the Middle East, the Far East, Africa, Latin America, the U.S.A., Australasia, etc.

Generalizations of this sort for whole countries are hazardous, and anyone with direct knowledge of any of them will no doubt be able to add qualifications to these impressionistic descriptions. But the total picture of a spreading secularization can hardly be denied; and the suggestion that it is possible (as in Sweden) to reach a limit of secularization beyond which the only progress is a turning back, has received confirmation from other accounts, notably the controversial description by Miss Kathleen Nott,[1] herself an acknowledged secular-humanist.

I have so far assumed that the word 'secular' ('secularization', etc.) is intelligible without a definition. Definitions have been offered:

> The withdrawal of areas of thought and life from religious – and finally also from metaphysical – control, and the attempt to understand and live in these areas in the terms which they alone offer.[2]

There is one. And Mr Denys Munby has described a secular society as one which, first, explicitly refuses to commit itself to any particular view of the nature of the

ference of the W.C.C. at Graz, January 1963, by S. Mackie, *Student World*, 1963, No. 1.

[1] K. Nott, *A Clean, Well-Lighted Place* (Heinemann, 1961); on Sweden.

[2] Charles West: cited in *Student World*, art. cit.

universe and the place of man in it; second, does not claim, or seek, to be homogeneous; and third, makes no attempt to enforce beliefs or to limit the expression of belief, i.e., is tolerant.[1] Note that these are almost entirely negative definitions. And the same impression is obtained if we look at particular features of a 'secular' society: e.g., education. As Mr Munby points out, such diverse thinkers as Coleridge, Newman, Pusey and F. D. Maurice were agreed a hundred years ago that (in the words of the last-named) theology is the ground on which all other studies stand.[2] By contrast, if we look at such a characteristic product of our time as the (1963) Report on Higher Education (the 'Robbins Report') we find, not merely that the word theology does not occur in the index – this is not surprising: nor do the words 'physics' or 'mathematics' – but that the word 'religion', which is not in the index, appears once, in common with other entities like politics, as an area to which a modern, Western democratic society guarantees freedom. The only over-arching concept in the Report, to which education in all its diversities is regarded as being committed, is the vaguely worded 'The Good Life'. And this is to be expected: this kind of modest commitment is the most that a secular society could offer as its positive delineation.

Christian writers have been arguing recently (Mr Munby is one of the clearest and most persuasive of them) that far from bemoaning the arrival of the secular society,

[1] Denys Munby, Riddell Lecture, *The Idea of a Secular Society* (O.U.P., 1963), ch. 1.

[2] Munby, op. cit., p. 79.

Christians should rejoice at it: for it is able to produce, more efficiently and with a greater professionalism, the kind of basis for the Good Life which Christian societies in the past have hoped to produce but failed – whether through amateurishness and ignorance, through half-heartedness and lack of concentration (part of the mind being elsewhere on higher things), or through positive dogmatic prejudice and *odium theologicum* – or indeed, through all three at once. It is not my intention to dispute this judgement. It may well be true. It is certainly likely to be influential, and one hopes influential in a salutary way, upon Christian thinking about secularism today. How far it will influence the thinking of 'secularists' themselves we cannot easily predict; perhaps more powerfully than they will be aware.

Indeed, it is possible that 'secularism' itself, especially its negative aspects, is much more an unconscious than a conscious process. It is possible that the unquestioned assumptions lying behind the architecture, the town-planning, the industrial organization and its economic priorities, the educational pyramid, the notions of social status, the grading of types of employment and their relative attractiveness, the images of advertisement, and the mythology of the hero (or the 'anti-hero') in film, TV, novel and drama – it is possible that the assumptions behind these are the really determinative forces in secularizing man. If so, it may be that a cool, rational attempt at assessing that secularization will have little effect in correcting its defects: it may be that one barely conscious image can only be replaced by another. Here the psychologist, and probably more cogently the imaginative artist, must take over. The present writer is neither.

In offering, therefore, a book which is largely about books, I am aware of the inadequacy (as well as the tedium) of the type of evidence chosen. Others could handle living, 'existential' evidence better. But books (and perhaps still more the lectures that lie behind so many of them) are still powerful in their persuasion – and in their dissuasion. If Christians are to understand – and perhaps to welcome – secularism, they must be aware of the writings that are so big a part of it. However, we shall all the time need to keep in the mind's eye the picture of people, places and things. And one of the pictures must be (since we cannot jump out of our historical skins) that of an absence. Perhaps a picture something like this:

> On the corner squatted a church – a huge casserole, fat, heavy and plain as the woman who prayed in it. Looking through the open doors as I passed, I saw the arches bending downward like a laborer under a heavy load. Even the bells of this church – presumably the voice of their god – were sour, and every Sunday morning I cursed them together with the priest who played some kind of chopsticks tune over and over on them. . . .
>
> The streets were almost deserted, since everyone was at dinner at the same time in Brooklyn. . . . The scene was made even more sententious by the fact that it was Sunday. There was a tremendous vacuum left behind by God.[1]

[1] Anatole Broyard, 'Sunday Dinner in Brooklyn', in G. Feldman and M. Gartenberg, *Protest* (Souvenir Press, 1959), pp. 22-5.

2

The Queen Deposed

›››◆‹‹‹

I. *The Spider and the Bee*

So thorough has been the 'Scientific Revolution' in the West that it is now almost impossible for a European man to think himself back into a time when theology not only claimed to be but was 'Queen of the Sciences'. It is usual to date the dethroning of this particular queen to the late sixteenth and early seventeenth century. And if a precise date is wanted, this is as good as any. Galileo put it as clearly as it has ever been stated, in his famous letter to the Grand Duchess Christina (written in 1613, and enlarged in 1614):

> I question whether there is not some equivocation in failing to specify the virtues which entitle sacred theology to the title of 'queen'. It might deserve that name by reason of including everything that is learned from all the other sciences and establishing everything by better methods and with profounder learning. . . . Or theology might be queen because of being occupied with a subject which excels in dignity all the subjects which compose the other sciences, and because her teachings are divulged in more sublime ways.
>
> That the title and authority of queen belongs to theology in the first sense, I think will not be affirmed by theologians who have any skill in the other sciences. None of these, I think, will say that geometry, astronomy, music and medicine

are more excellently contained in the Bible than they are in the books of Archimedes, Ptolemy, Boethius and Galen. Hence it seems likely that regal pre-eminence is given to theology in the second sense; that is, by reason of its subject and the miraculous communication, by divine revelation, of conclusions which could not be conceived by men in any other way, concerning chiefly the attainment of eternal blessedness.

Let us grant, then, that theology is conversant with the loftiest divine contemplation, and occupies the regal throne among the sciences by this dignity. But acquiring the highest authority in this way, if she does not descend to the lower and humbler speculations of the subordinate sciences and has no regard for them therefore they are not concerned with blessedness, then her professors should not arrogate to themselves the authority to decide on controversies in professions which they have neither studied nor practised. Why, this would be as if an absolute despot, being neither a physician nor an architect, but knowing himself free to command, should undertake to administer medicines and erect buildings according to his whim – at grave peril of his poor patients' lives, and the speedy collapse of his edifices.[1]

We all know what happened to Galileo's own astronomical findings, as a result of the Church's ignoring his warnings about the competence of the 'Queen of the Sciences' in this matter. On 24th February, 1616, eleven Consultants appointed by Pope Paul V, all of them theologians with not a mathematician among them, declared: 1. That the Proposition 'that the sun is the centre of the world and devoid of local motion' is 'foolish and absurd

[1] Translation in Stillman Drake, *Discoveries and Opinions of Galileo* (Doubleday, 1957), p. 192: cited in A. Koestler, *The Sleepwalkers* (Hutchinson, 1959), p. 435.

philosophically, and formally heretical'; and 2. That the Proposition that 'the earth is not the centre of the world nor immovable, but moves as a whole, and also with a diurnal motion', 'merited the same censure in philosophy, and that from a theological standpoint, it was at least erroneous in the faith'.[1]

It may seem otiose to dig up again this notorious controversy, but it presents the issue in the clearest, if crudest, forms. And the issue can occur again, in different forms and under different circumstances. It is, for instance, a little disturbing to find a contemporary Jesuit historian defending the Jesuits of the seventeenth century in the following terms. In his admirable biography of Cardinal Robert Bellarmine, Fr James Brodrick points out that many of the mathematicians of the Jesuit College in Rome were actually in agreement with Galileo. But after all, he says, they were

> first and foremost religious, vowed to the sanctification of their own souls and, as a result of that, apostles dedicated to the promotion of the greater glory of God by striving to bring about, aided by divine grace, the supernatural salvation of their fellow men. . . . They were not founded to promote science, poetry, music or anything else, except in so far as such pursuits might advance the glory of God and the sanctification of their own and other men's souls. Consequently, though the mathematicians of the Roman College were delighted by Galileo's discoveries, they were far from sharing his optimism about the imminent triumph of heliocentrism. The traditional mould of human thinking could be suddenly broken only with danger to spiritual

[1] James Brodrick, S.J., *Robert Bellarmine* (Burns & Oates, 1961), p. 273.

interests far exceeding in importance any concern for strict scientific truth.[1]

This distinction between 'scientific truth' and 'supernatural salvation', and subordination of the former to the latter, surely implies the kind of theological separation (*apartheid*, shall we call it?) from which the scientific revolution, among other things, happily delivered us.

But if we single out the well-known episode of Galileo's condemnation as a crucial case, we must not let it conceal from us the fact that the scientific revolution had started long before, and went on developing long after. One of the most distinguished philosophers of science has traced its beginnings back, certainly, into the thirteenth and fourteenth centuries. Among the original contributions to the development of natural science in Europe in the Middle Ages he lists the following:

1. In scientific method, there was the recovery of the idea of rational explanation; and in particular, the use of mathematics raised the problem how to verify (and to falsify) theories. This was solved by the Scholastic theory of induction and the experimental method. (He mentions especially optics and magnetics in the thirteenth and fourteenth centuries.)

2. There was an extension of mathematics to the whole of physical science (in principle). Aristotle had subordinated mathematics to 'physics' (his sense); now the scientists were less interested in the 'physical' or metaphysical question of 'cause', and more interested to ask questions which could be answered by mathematical

[1] Brodrick, op. cit., p. 340.

theory and which were within reach of experimental verification. (He mentions statics, optics and astronomy, thirteenth and fourteenth centuries.)

3. There was extremely rapid advance in technology – animal-, water- and wind-power; the mechanical clock, magnifying lenses, measuring instruments, etc. There was a new approach to questions of space and motion at the end of the thirteenth century. And knowledge of biology was extended, in medicine, flora and fauna, and classification.

4. But perhaps most important were two contributions to the purpose and nature of science itself. First, the idea (first explicitly expressed in the thirteenth century) that the purpose of science is to gain power over nature – a power useful to man. And second, the idea insisted on by theology,

> that neither God's action nor man's speculation could be constrained within any particular system of scientific philosophy or thought. . . . The effect of this idea on natural science was to bring out the relativity of all scientific theories and the fact that they might be replaced by others more successful in fulfilling the requirements of the rational and experimental methods.[1]

Professor Crombie points out that this would gradually have the effect of destroying from within, and bursting the bonds of Aristotelian cosmology and physics. There was, inevitably, a resistance to it among late scholastics, especially those who linked the old system to theology, and those 'whose humanism had given them too great

[1] A. C. Crombie, *Augustine to Galileo* (Falcon, 1952), p. 273.

a devotion to the ancient texts'. (This connection between 'humanism' and reaction is interesting, in view of the use of the word 'humanist' in the twentieth century.) But Crombie's conclusion seems inescapable: that it was 'the growth of these thirteenth- and fourteenth-century experimental and mathematical methods that brought about the movement which by the seventeenth century had become so striking as to be called the Scientific Revolution'.[1]

We can see two of these characteristics emerging most clearly and explicitly in Francis Bacon. In the Preface to his *Great Instauration* (or new Method) Bacon said that he was 'labouring to lay the foundation, not of any sect or doctrine, but of human utility and power' – i.e. power over nature. And this could even be given a biblical interpretation: as Crombie puts it, 'The object of the Great Instauration . . . was to show how to win back that dominion, which had been lost at the Fall.'[2] And this leads Bacon to that combination of the inductive and the deductive methods which his medieval predecessors (including his great namesake, Roger) had evolved. Bacon compares this combination (i.e. of observation with generalized rules) to the work of the bee. He has been comparing (in his *Novum Organum*) men of experiment (today we should call them 'the empiricists') with men of dogma (a hundred and fifty years ago we should have called them the 'rationalists'). The former are like ants: they merely collect and use. The latter,

[1] Crombie, op. cit., p. 273. [2] Ibid., p. 388.

the reasoners resemble spiders, who make cobwebs out of their own substance. But the bee takes the middle course, it gathers its material from the flowers of the garden and of the field, but transforms and digests it by a power of its own.[1]

This last, he says, is the true business of the 'philosopher'.

From Francis Bacon onward we see the bee increasingly replacing the spider. (The ant, who is the technologist, still of course has his place, but his task is the limited one of collecting and using.) The result is, of course, a notion of science that is essentially hypothetical and conceptual. And it is precisely this 'conceptual' nature of scientific theories that makes scientific growth possible. To rest in dogmatism is to arrest advance.

But the 'queen' continued to be most reluctant to let her crown go. Again the story is a familiar one: Descartes pretending to ultimate doubt, but bringing God in as the connecting link between 'mind' and 'extension'; Paley arguing from mechanism to a Great Mechanic; biologists using organic adaptation to show the wisdom of God in the works of his creation – and thereby opening the way for the argument from 'dysteleology' (or lack of adaptation) to atheism, which has remained the most powerful argument ever since; and Newton introducing God into his physical theories to restore the balance of the solar system which he believed to be in slight disequilibrium – and thus exposing himself

to the retort, after Laplace showed that the solar system in

[1] Crombie, op. cit., p. 401, quoting Bacon, *Novum Organum* I, aphor. 95 (1620).

fact maintained its own equilibrium, that the hypothesis of God was no longer necessary.[1]

It is understandable that the 'argument from design' remained so long (and still remains, in some Christian circles) the most popular argument for the existence of a Powerful Planner behind the universe. The only Christian theologian or philosopher of religion who got mentioned in the Reith Lectures delivered by Professor P. Medawar[2] was Paley – mentioned only in order to be dismissed; and in the correspondence which followed, Professor Medawar seemed a little surprised, though pleased, to learn that Paley was also out of fashion among Christians now. However, it should be clear, to Christians and non-Christians alike, that the time is gone when we can take seriously the kind of 'proof' typified by the following charming passage in the *Antidote against Atheism* of the seventeenth-century Cambridge Platonist, Henry More:

> I demand therefore concerning the cock why he has spurs at all, or having them, how they came to be so fittingly placed. For he might have had none, or so misplaced that they had been utterly useless, and so his pleasure in fighting had been to no purpose. . . . I might add to these that Nature has made the hindmost parts of our body which we sit upon most fleshly, as providing for our ease and making us a natural cushion. . . . So that it is manifest that a divine Providence strikes through all things.[3]

[1] Crombie, op. cit., p. 402.

[2] P. B. Medawar, *The Future of Man* (Methuen, 1960).

[3] H. More, *Antidote against Atheism* (1653/5): cited in J. Laird, Gifford Lectures, *Theism and Cosmology* (Allen & Unwin, 1940), p. 262.

Bernardin de St Pierre (the author of *Paul et Virginie*) went even further, and suggested that the Almighty in his Providence took thought even for man's more frivolous moments: in *Études de la Nature* he suggested that melons have ribs so that they may be conveniently divided up at family parties.[1] And it is only a refinement of this crude 'teleological argument for the existence of God' which reappears in this century in such works as Sir James Jeans' *The Mysterious Universe* or Eddington's *The Nature of the Physical World*, hinting that only a God who was a super-Mathematician could have thought up the complicated cosmos in which we exist. But the non-sequiturs in the argument have been demonstrated so many times by philosophers, from Kant onwards, that it would not be easy today to find anyone with a trained philosophical mind who would defend it. It is not only the philosophers who are dissatisfied with it: one of the neatest demolitions of the argument occurs, more or less by accident, in an amusing contemporary playlet, *A Resounding Tinkle*, by the young dramatist, N. F. Simpson. His two Comedians are discussing how easily customers feel cheated:

First Comedian . . . I've known people feel cheated about some odd things. I've known people buy a bath sponge and do calculations to show that two-thirds of the sponge is made up of holes. And it galls them to think that two-thirds of what they've paid good money for isn't really there. . . .

Second Comedian Not with a sponge. They've no right to feel cheated over a sponge. A sponge is where you expect

[1] Bernardin de St Pierre, *Études de la Nature*: cited in W. R. Thompson, *Science and Common Sense* (Longmans, 1937), p. 129.

to find holes. . . . The holes are there for a purpose in a sponge. They're there to soak up the water.

First C. Now you're bringing a new element into it. Start talking about purpose and you'll have the whole argument bedevilled. Before you know where we are we shall be splitting hairs. No. Leave purpose out of it. They're not there to soak up the water. The holes in a sponge soak up the water. It's not the same.

Second C. Which is what I said in the first place. The holes are there for a purpose.

First C. Purpose purpose purpose! It isn't purpose. It's coincidence. They happen to be there long before you or anybody ever used a sponge in a bath. And that goes for everything else. . . . What, for instance, is the purpose of the sea? Is it so that sponges can have somewhere to grow? To give fish somewhere to use their gills? Perhaps you want to tell me that oceans exist to cater for submarines? Rather than waste all those submarines on dry land, God in His all-seeing wisdom made the sea. That's how you're arguing. You're arguing from effect back to cause and it's disastrous. . . . All I'm trying to say is that anyone who starts with the idea of a sponge, and starts squeezing water over himself out of it before he lets his mind wander slowly back through the millennia to the beginning of things, is going the wrong way about it. He'll end up in a paroxysm of wonder. He'll want to start worshipping something on the spot, while he's still dripping with water and his glasses are steamed up. And for no better reason . . . than that the entire evolutionary processes of the cosmos seem to him to have been geared for several million years to the task of providing him with something to wash with. How marvellous are Thy ways, O Lord! The seasons always working out just right for the crops; the flowers never forgetting what colour they have to be to attract the right kind of insect and repel the wrong kind, blessed be God! Isn't it wonderful the way it all works out? And if it had worked out quite differently that would have been pretty wonderful too.[1]

II. *A Shrinking World*

If philosophers have demonstrated that no argument from within the material that science deals with can prove the existence of a God 'outside' science; and if science can in fact get on with its job effectively without requiring the hypothesis of a God; then, since our contemporary world is increasingly shaped and controlled by scientific categories it is obvious that a 'secular' state will be the most natural accompaniment of a scientific society. And in fact, if one examines the behaviour of practising scientists it seems clear that any 'religious' or 'theological' or 'metaphysical' views that they may hold, and sincerely hold, tend to bear much the same relationship to their work in the laboratory as their lesiure-time activities in general – viz., a merely marginal one. A biochemist will probably be a better biochemist if he plays golf on his day-off, as this exercise and brain-relaxation will improve his scientific performance. So too, it could be argued that a scientist who has a personal religious faith, and indeed perhaps preserves his sanity by his weekly participation in corporate worship, will be a better scientist than if he neglected this religious activity. But the connection between the two activities remains indirect and largely therapeutic. And perhaps the marginal nature of the relationship can be shown

[1] N. F. Simpson, *A Resounding Tinkle*: from *Observer Plays* (Faber, 1958), pp. 233-4.

even more clearly by looking at other societies than our own, societies in which we cannot say that the scientific activity is merely divorced from any 'religious' activity, for there is no religious activity for it to be divorced from, or to which it can even be marginally related.

The isolation of China from the rest of the world began to be broken down in the nineteenth century, when a few students were sent to Europe, for educational purposes. The Chinese authorities were impressed by the efficiency of the Western powers – particularly, of course, their military efficiency from which the Chinese had suffered. A Chinese graduate of Yale in 1854 returned to China with enthusiasm for Western education, and became a promoter of educational reform. Finally the Manchu officials were persuaded to start a scheme for sending students regularly to America or Europe, and the first batch of thirty were sent to America in 1872. The scheme was suppressed later by reactionaries, but the effects of it continued, and were multiplied by the fall of the Manchu dynasty and the setting up of a Chinese republic in 1912. Although the republic was abortive, the 'Chinese Renaissance' movement, especially among students, went from strength to strength. Some of its most ardent advocates urged a complete severance from Chinese culture and tradition. One of them, Ch'en Tu-hsiu said that

> Whether in politics, scholarship, morality or literature, the Western method and the Chinese method are two absolutely different things and can in no way be com-

promised or reconciled. We need not now discuss which is better and which is worse, as that is a separate issue. But we must first decide on the national policy whether we should continue to use the old Chinese method or to adopt the new Western method. If we decide to be conservative, then we must use the old Chinese method through and through, and need not waste our money to send students abroad or open any schools for the study of Western learning. But if we decide to reform, then we must adopt the new Western method in all things and need not confuse the issue by such nonsense as 'national heritage' or 'special circumstances'. . . .[1]

And, in answering charges of subversive teaching he declares frankly that

In order to support Mr Democracy, we are obliged to oppose Confucianism, the code of rituals, chastity, traditional ethics, old politics; and in order to support Mr Science we are compelled to oppose traditional arts, traditional religion; and in order to support Mr Democracy and Mr Science, we just have to oppose the so-called national heritage and old literature.[2]

The attack on religion was central to this Chinese renaissance movement. The Emperor had traditionally stood between the Supreme Power in the universe (for which the terms used were either *T'ien*=Heaven, or *Shang Ti*=Lord on High) and the people, and as the Son of Heaven he had divine authority to rule. But when the monarchy was abolished in 1911, with it went the most powerful support for belief in Heaven. Here are a few statements made by educated Chinese about this time:

[1] Wen-Han Kiang, *The Chinese Student Movement* (O.U.P., 1948), p. 24.
[2] Ibid., p. 25.

T'ien or *Shang Ti* in Chinese means exactly the same as God in English. But the God-idea is now discredited by the educated people. We do not believe in a personal God any more.

To us, the *T'ien* or *Shang Ti* is a collective (noun) and stands for all that is mysterious and unexplained. The ancients were surrounded by mysteries and they had no means of understanding them and so invented the belief in the existence of a mysterious being which they called *T'ien* or *Shang Ti*. The idea has persisted to this day because it has been found a useful means of social control. The ignorant classes have no self-control. The 'personal God' idea excites fear and so acts as restraint upon their conduct. As to the reference in the Classics about the justice of Heaven, of rewards and punishments, that is only a way of writing or speaking. There is in nature the law of cause and effect, which works positively, and so there is no necessity for postulating a Personal Being in the universe dispensing rewards and punishments.[1]

There were dissentient voices: not only of traditionalists, but also of some who had indeed been to the West, but found it noisy, empty, competitive and unspiritual. But the influential and powerful scholar, Hu Shih, dismissed all such talk, such glorification of the East against the materialistic West:

After all, there is not much spirituality in a civilization which bound the feet of its women for almost a thousand years without a protest, nor in that other civilization which long tolerated the practice of *suttee* or cremation of widows and has maintained the horrible caste system to this day.

And by contrast with this, he says:

[1] Wen-Han Kiang, op. cit., pp. 47-8.

> On the other hand, that civilization which makes the fullest possible use of human ingenuity and intelligence in search of truth in order to control nature and transform matter for the service of mankind, to liberate the human spirit from ignorance, superstition, and slavery to the forces of nature, and to reform social and political institutions for the benefit of the greatest number – such a civilization is highly idealistic and spiritual.[1]

This, written in 1923, might be taken as an encomium of the Welfare State in Great Britain in the nineteen fifties and sixties.

It is not, then, surprising to learn that in the middle of this Chinese renaissance movement the Ministry of Education invited three distinguished Western thinkers to lecture in Pekin: Professor John Dewey of Columbia University in 1919, and, in 1920, Mr Bertrand Russell from Cambridge and Dr Paul Munroe also from Columbia.

> Professor Dewey . . . was the great apostle of philosophic liberalism and experimental methodology, the advocate of complete freedom of thought, and the man who above all other teachers equated education to the practical problems of civic co-operation and useful living. Dr Munroe (who had had great experience in secondary education) was to examine into the state of the schools. Mr Russell came as the foremost exponent of a critical attitude to the old, a scientist [*sic*] who knew how to evolve from his science a philosophy of life and the universe.[2]

It was Professor John Dewey who made the deepest impression, and had the most lasting influence. But we can

[1] Wen-Han Kiang, op. cit., p. 44.

[2] E. R. Hughes, *The Invasion of China by the Western World* (Black, 1937), pp. 182-3.

hardly doubt that Mr Bertrand Russell also powerfully supplemented the anti-religious elements in the movement; so that we are not at all surprised to find Hu Shih saying, in 1931, that 'Practically all the prominent leaders of thought in China today are openly agnostics and even atheists. And the young men are even openly anti-religious.'[1]

But this could not last, and it is indicative of the shallowness of the Western pragmatists, utilitarians and positivists who visited China at this time that they could not see that it wouldn't last. Bertrand Russell, in his own book on China written after his visit, saw that 'The Chinese, even the most modern, look to the white nations, especially America, for moral maxims to replace those of Confucius'. But what is his reaction to this demand? The cynical response 'They have not yet grasped that men's morals in the mass are the same everywhere: they do as much harm as they dare, and as much good as they must.'[2] And he even concludes, with a complacency that is rendered more astonishing by subsequent events, that 'the hegemony of Russia in Asia would not, to my mind, be in any way regrettable'. And so all he could offer the Chinese, to slake their moral and metaphysical thirst, was scientific know-how, and a slow and unexciting attempt to catch up with the democratic processes of the West. John Dewey, whose influence was greater, failed to see (as the historian

[1] Wen-Han Kiang, op. cit., p. 48.

[2] A. de Riencourt, *The Soul of China* (Cape, 1959), pp. 207f., quoting B. Russell, *The Problem of China*, p. 81.

Amaury de Riencourt has put it) China's desire for 'an all-embracing formula, a philosophic panacea which would have universal value'. Confucius had held that 'one single principle suffices to understand all'. Dewey, with his American pragmatism, rejected any notion that there were universal solutions for mankind's ills. And thus many of the Chinese intellectuals came to reject the Dewey-Russell contribution, and, like Ch'en Tu-hsiu, to turn to Marxism. Indeed, as de Riencourt puts it, it was Marxism that 'restored China's traditional way of thinking'.

The alliance between a scientific-secular movement and an anti-religious revolt was easily predictable in a China where the religion was a confused amalgam of Confucian ethics with popular Buddhist and Taoist elements, and was in any case closely tied to a political and social order that was itself collapsing. When, however, we look at twentieth-century Russia we might have expected to find a slightly different situation. For the Marxist challenge to religion was based on a social-historical argument that, at its best, was profounder, and ultimately more revolutionary, than the rather crude 'materialism' and 'scientific rationalism' which prevailed for the time among the Chinese intellectuals. And yet in fact at the ordinary levels of day-to-day argument and thought the average Russian communist seems to have continued to make the same somewhat naive assumptions about the omni-competence of science, and the resulting absurdity of 'religion'. Generalizations of this sort are, of course, hazardous. But some confirmation for this one can be found in the reflections of a French (Roman Catholic) priest, Russian-speaking, who visited Russia in 1961, and the account of whose experiences have not received much notice in this country.[1] Père René Girault says:

I think of my conversation with Yuri: 'No intelligent man is a believer here', he said. 'Just look at those you find in Church: all old women, and the uneducated.' He explained to me that his mother is a believer, that she has tried sending believers to see him, to try and bring him back to the faith. 'But', he said, almost sadly, 'they were nearly all ignorant folk, knowing nothing of science. . . .'

I asked him whether he had really found in his system the answer to problems posed by life and the meaning of life. His reply was frank, and sums up an attitude which is not without nobility: 'I don't want to hide from you that often I do experience a deep disquiet (*angoisse*) . . . because I ask myself questions to which science has just now no answer. . . . But I'd much rather stay in my disquiet and in science, which is looking for truth, than give myself an artificial consolation, blinding myself with religion, like an opium.'

I could only answer him, as I answered others: 'If religion were what you think it is, certainly I myself would have nothing to do with it. . . . But religion is something quite different, and it is the friend of science.' But he replied: 'Here there's not a single priest, not a single believer who is on the side of science.'[2]

This was only one among many conversations that Fr Girault had.

All the atheists I met – I can only summarize the numerous conversations I had with them – were very ready to enter into discussion with me, and kept it up even when, after a

[1] René Girault in *Lumière et Vie* (Paris), Dec. 1961. [2] Ibid., p. 90.

few minutes, they found that they were talking to a believer, even more, with a '*sviatchennik*' (priest). Only they were exceptionally astonished, and sometimes even visibly bowled-over, to find that the person talking to them apparently united in himself these two incompatible realities: science and religion. This incompatibility is in fact one of the most fundamental principles of Marxism. And it is painful to have to state that the Orthodox Church seems hardly to have any desire to reply to these objections – this is the penalty that has to be paid for persecution, or else is sheer inattention to the problems.

He points out how difficult it is to estimate the number of 'believers', since to profess Christianity has grave inconveniences in social life: so that

the age of believers roughly corresponds to the age when workers are entitled to retire (fifty-five or sixty years old); before that, for reasons which one can't exactly call very courageous, but which have a good many extenuating circumstances to them, many people are in the position of being believers without daring to run the risk of practising their faith.[1]

But it is his conclusion on the relative appeal of atheism and Marxism which is most relevant to our theme. He speaks of the reality of 'the phenomenon of atheism', and observes:

It is easy to talk disparagingly (*dénoncer*) of the feebleness and elementary nature of anti-religious literature. It remains true that it is extraordinarily harmful, and that an over-simple apologetics is a poor answer to it. Atheism is a much wider phenomenon than communism, and it sometimes happens that the latter pushes it in front of itself, even when

[1] René Girault, op. cit. p. 95.

it does not itself overtake it. A friend I met at Varsovie, on my return from Russia, said to me, speaking of his own country: 'If the present situation continues in Poland, we shan't become communists, but there'll be plenty of atheists.' Faced with the questions which contemporary atheism poses to the Bible and the history of the Church, we've simply got to understand that our apologetics must be extremely vigilant, and that any of it that is dated must be completely refashioned.[1]

An illuminating contrast between contemporary Soviet unbelief and Anglo-Saxon agnosticism was revealed during the visit which the Russian poet, Yevgeny Yevtushenko, paid to Cambridge in 1962, with Mr Kingsley Amis as his cicerone. Mr Amis describes how

After lunch we went across to King's chapel. Yevtushenko's height and youth and foreign look gave him an authority which had nothing to do with arrogance. In the way he looked about him I thought I detected the courteous interest, the concern to see but not to make comparisons, of a man looking at something impressive that the Other Side had done.

'You atheist?' he asked me in English.

'Well yes, but it's more that I hate him.'

I felt he understood me very fully. He gave his delightful grin. There was in it a superiority impossible to resent. (It might be real.)

'Me', he said, pointing to himself, then gesturing more vaguely towards the roof, the other people there, the Rubens, but also seeming to include the being I had just mentioned; 'me . . . means nothing'.[2]

[1] René Girault, op. cit., pp. 97-8.

[2] Kingsley Amis, 'Kipling Good' in *Spectator* (London), No. 6993, 6th July, 1962, p. 13.

III. *The Secular State*

We have seen the scientific revolution and the secular state arriving more or less hand in hand. But it may be argued that they did not always arrive simultaneously; that their partnership is accidental; and that 'secular' can in fact exist, and has co-existed with a theological outlook. Once the Queen has abdicated, if she remains on good terms with the management, she can be offered an honorary seat in the Upper House. It is only where she has had a reputation for outstanding tyranny, or refused to abdicate and had to be forcibly deposed, or continues clandestine political and subversive activity, that she has to be liquidated: i.e., the state has to be not merely secular but secularist. It is well-known that on the whole secular societies are only 'anti-clerical' in those places where the Church has previously had totalitarian claims. And this is true not only of the Christian Church but of other religions. The vigour and uncompromising 'secularism' of the young Renaissance movement in China fifty years ago was due not merely to the excitement of the new discoveries of Western science and technology, but to the all-inclusive oppressiveness of the Manchu theocracy. The same was, of course, true of Revolutionary France, of Mexico, of the Philippines, etc. By contrast, it is interesting to study the régime in Independent (South) Korea. The Nationalist and Liberatory movement, from the beginning of this century, was almost wholly 'religion-inspired'. In the 'Conspiracy Trial' of 1912, Baron Yun and many others of those arrested and accused of treasonous, anti-Japanese activity were Korean Christians; and the great 'Declaration of Independence' on 1st March, 1919, was launched by three religious groups – of the thirty-three signatories of the Declaration (all of whom gave themselves up to the police voluntarily and were imprisoned with extreme brutality) fifteen were Christians (mostly Korean preachers, Methodist or Presbyterian), fifteen were members of 'Chundoism' (a syncretic 'Religion of the Heavenly Path') and three were Buddhists. Whatever may have happened to the Korean independence movement later, due to the personal moving to the Right of Dr Syngman Rhee and above all to the partition of the country into North and South, the early days of the movement were anything but 'secularist'. Nevertheless, this alliance between Christianity and 'liberatory' movements, though on the face of it it may look like a stirring expression of Christian social purpose, is not without its dangers. One reason for the early popularity of Christianity in Vietnam was the fact that the Roman Catholic leaders among the Vietnamese were prominent in supporting Vietnamese nationalism and ending French imperialism in Indo-China. (South Vietnam has the highest proportion of Catholics in the Far East, next after the Philippines – ten per cent of the population.) Yet, as has been seen during the fateful months of 1963, the results have been disquieting. Even before the outbreak of open rebellion by the 'Buddhists' against the Dien régime, there were reports, as early as March 1963, of complaints by the majority (mostly 'Buddhist') of the population that Catholic religious processions monopolize the streets and block the traffic; and the non-Catholic populace were objecting to being woken at 5 a.m. by church bells! And there was the extraordinary paradox that the official state philosophy adopted was Emanuel Mounier's 'Personalism'; and that non-Christian citizens were being invited to lecture-courses in order to be indoctrinated, even 'brain-washed' into Personalism! (This report came from a Vietnamese Roman Catholic lady.[1]) The end of the régime was inevitable.

Of course the Roman Catholic Church in other parts of the world has been quick to disown this particular 'Catholic' phenomenon. And the most recent Roman Catholic views on 'toleration' in other parts of the world show a revolutionary advance. Nevertheless those who are not Roman Catholics feel that more penitence should be expressed for past versions of 'Catholic power'. It cannot be denied that there has been justification for the secularist suspicion that the Queen will never willingly relinquish her throne. The famous exposition of the official Roman Catholic attitude towards toleration of 'non-Catholics' seems quite unambiguous:

The Roman Catholic Church, convinced, through its divine prerogative, of being the only true church, must demand the right of freedom for herself alone, because such a right can only be possessed by truth, never by error. As to other religions, the Church will certainly never draw the sword, but she will require that by legitimate means they shall not be allowed to propagate false doctrine. Consequently,

[1] See *Informations Catholiques Internationales*, No. 188, 15 Mar., 1962.

in a state where the majority of the people are Catholic, the Church will require that legal existence be denied to error, and that if religious minorities actually exist, they shall have only a *de facto* existence without opportunity to spread their beliefs. . . . In some countries, Catholics will be obliged to ask full religious freedom for all, resigned at being forced to cohabitate where they alone should rightfully be allowed to live. But in doing this the Church does not renounce her thesis, which remains the most imperative of her laws, but merely adapts herself to *de facto* conditions, which must be taken into account in practical affairs.[1]

The disquiet which many Roman Catholics feel about this doctrine is an index of the changing mood within the Roman Church; and this mood is even reflected at official levels, since Pope John XXIII. But so long as the attitude survives anywhere in the Church, the appearance of books like Paul Blanshard, *Freedom and Catholic Power* (Secker, 1951), Avro Manhattan, *The Catholic Church Against the Twentieth Century* (Watts, 1947), or Tom Truman, *Catholic Action And Politics* (Merlin Press, 1960), however crude and unfair in detail they may be, are inevitable.

Not, of course, that the existence of a secular state which tolerates within it various minority religious groups, is without problems of its own. America is a good example of a state which, though publicly secular is avowedly non-secularist, and indeed contains religious, if not specifically Christian elements in its very Constitution. Americans would mostly reject the suggestion

[1] *Civiltà Catholica*, April 1948: cited in *Christian Century*, 23rd June, 1948. But contrast the fine encyclical *Pacem in Terris* (1962).

that the separation of Church and state, guaranteed by the First Amendment, implied that America was a secularist society. But the problems of what tolerance implies are still there. Roman Catholics, for instance, have long pleaded that since they contribute to state taxes, some of the money from the taxes should be used, not merely for 'public' (i.e., secular) schools, which Roman Catholic children may not (or at least, strictly should not) attend, but also for 'private' (i.e., in this case, Roman Catholic) schools. This plea has been steadily rejected. But in some States free bus transport to take children to Roman Catholic schools, and also aid towards some of the text-books required in school, have been voted from public funds. A Supreme Court case in 1947 ruled that both these were permissible and not excluded by the First Amendment. On the other hand, a celebrated case which came before the Supreme Court in March 1948 (the McCollum case), though it did not lead to any reversal of the previous ruling (that public money could be used for transport and text-books for private schools), laid down clearly that school-rooms in public schools might not be used for classes released under the conscience clause for 'private' religious instruction; and what was more important, the general argument of the judges, accepted even by those who dissented from the actual judgement, was that 'The First Amendment has erected a wall between Church and State which must be kept high and impregnable'.[1]

[1] Cited in P. Blanshard, *Freedom and Catholic Power* (Secker, 1951), pp. 86, 91.

But it is not only the Roman Catholic Church which raises these problems for an officially secular state. On 26th June, 1962 there were headlines in all the American papers, to the effect: 'Supreme Court bans School Prayers'. Behind this dramatic (and perhaps slightly oversimplified) statement there was quite a tangle of judgements, dissensions and contradictory arguments. Back in 1955 the County Council of San Bernardino County (California) asked whether prayer might be used every day in public schools. In Washington it had been ruled in 1909 that

> a public school teacher had no legal right to open school each morning with a prayer, since prayer is a religious exercise and is constitutionally forbidden.

And the Attorney General gave the same advice to San Bernardino County:

> In the great ideological struggle in which the world is now engaged, enforced conformity of thought is not a weapon which our side may use – it is rather one of the evils against which we fight. . . . Faith is important – it is at the very foundation of our cause – but it is faith dictated by the heart, not faith dictated by the state.

So when the mother of a school child in Maryland in 1961 challenged the school board's right to use the Lord's Prayer at school assembly, precedent should have shown what the decision was likely to be. Nevertheless, the Maryland Court of Appeals first ruled that the rights of pupil and parents were not violated by this practice. But the case was taken up to the Supreme Court. As was also a similar case in Pennsylvania: a parent complained that the reading of ten verses from the Bible, read daily by a student at a school over the amplifying system, was a violation of the First Amendment – and a Federal court agreed with this.

The First Amendment says, 1. 'That Congress shall make no law respecting an establishment of religion'; but 2. '. . . nor prohibiting the free exercise thereof'. And legal counsel for the Maryland school board argued that since the Lord's Prayer was nondenominational, the use of it could not be regarded as an attempt to 'establish' a religion; indeed, that the forbidding of its use was 'prohibiting the free exercise' of a religious belief of the majority of American citizens. But his argument was disallowed by the Court. One dissentient judge alone (Justice Potter Stewart) argued that there were many governmental practices that reflect American religious traditions. These are not the establishment of a religion, but a recognition of 'the deeply entrenched and highly cherished spiritual traditions of our nation'. But the majority were clear that the Founding Fathers believed

> that religion is too personal, too sacred, too holy to permit its unhallowed perversion by a civil magistrate. . . . The prayer of each man from his soul must be his and his alone. That is the genius of the First Amendment. If there is anything clear in the First Amendment, it is that the right of the people to pray in their own way is not to be controlled by the election returns. (Justice Black.)

However, Black continued:

> There is, of course, nothing in the decision reached here that is inconsistent with the fact that school children are

officially encouraged to express love for our country by reciting historical documents such as the Declaration of Independence which contains references to the Deity, or by singing espoused anthems which include the composer's professions of faith in a Supreme Being, or with the fact that there are many manifestations in our public life of belief of God.

This suggested a possible way out to some state education authorities who were not willing to be totally secularized by the Supreme Court decision. Some of the school boards decided to ignore the decision: in Atlanta, and Rocky Mount, North Carolina there were categorical statements, such as 'We will not pay any attention to the Supreme Court ruling'; and the President of the Hicksville school board said they had 'no intention of abolishing prayer. If we are compelled to ban it, then we'll devise another prayer. A school without prayers is not a school. . . . Not to have a prayer is a violation of our religious freedom.' But those who took the Supreme Court more seriously decided to connect school prayer with patriotism. In New York City many schools abandoned prayer recitation and Bible reading, but began the school day with the first stanza of *America*. Hicksville, Long Island, when told that their school must obey the Supreme Court ruling, voted that the pupils would recite as a prayer the fourth verse of the National Anthem:

Blest with victory and peace, may the Heav'n-rescued land
Praise the Power that hath made and preserved us a nation!
Then conquer we must, when our cause it is just,
And this be our motto, 'In God is our trust!'

But again two parents objected that they did not 'desire a return to God in public school'; and that though they had no objection to the Anthem being sung it must not be treated as a prayer. Their objection was sustained. One suggestion in other schools was that if prayers were no longer allowed to be recited, a period for silent meditation could not constitutionally be objected to. But one educationist said he thought there were 'valid reservations as to the educational value of a practice in which the teacher cannot have a positive and direct role'; and an attorney, who had defended prayer in the Supreme Court case, observed sarcastically that 'It is now constitutional to remain silent'. In the case itself counsel for Maryland and Pennsylvania argued that the Lord's Prayer and Bible reading were not held for 'religious purposes': ten verses from the Bible were read to give the pupils ethical and moral instruction. Counsel for Maryland went so far as to argue that the recitation of the Lord's Prayer was not religious: the morning exercises had a calming effect on the pupils and resulted in better behaviour during school hours. Mr Justice Stewart suggested that Baltimore might try tranquillizer pills.

The whole controversy,[1] as it appears on paper[2] and looked at from a great distance, cannot but appear faintly comic. But at least it illustrates both the difficulties of

[1] Which has been finally decided by the Supreme Court (one dissentient Judge): the Lord's Prayer and Bible readings are *un*-constitutional (17th June, 1963: *Guardian*, 18th June, 1963).

[2] Article by Theodore Powell, *Saturday Review of Literature*, 20th April, 1963, pp. 62-78.

maintaining a consistent line between secular and secularist, and the ardent, even finicky, concern of American democracy to maintain tolerance along with 'anti-establishmentarianism'.

Perhaps the most interesting, because the most recent, attempt at a state which is secular without being secularist, is to be found in India. When partition became inevitable, there were many Hindus who wanted to emulate Islam by making India 'Hindustan' comparable to Pakistan: Should not the Hindu Dharma be the basis of the new nation? The *Rashtriya Swayam Sevak* was the movement which pressed this most strongly, urging 'Wasn't England a Protestant state, with Catholics suffering disabilities? Catholicism is the religion of Eire, etc.; Hindus are 310 millions out of 360 millions (1961 figures): Why should they deny themselves a pre-eminent position to placate the Muslim minority? . . .' But Gandhiji, and the Congress he had shaped, was opposed to this. The Indian tradition had always been one of toleration of many religions and sects. As Dr Pannikar observes caustically:

> the doctrine of the religious State . . . was never a part of Indian tradition. The expulsion of the Moors, the Test Acts and exclusion of Dissenters, the Revocation of the Edict of Nantes and other such manifestations of the doctrine of a single community enjoying political power in the State is a Christian conception developed in Europe.[1]

[1] K. M. Pannikar, *The Foundations of a New India* (Allen & Unwin, 1963), p. 163.

And he defines the 'composite secular state' as follows:

> Political institutions must be based on the economic and social interests of the entire community, without reference to religion, race or sect: that all must enjoy equal rights, but no privileges, prescriptive rights or special claims should be allowed for any group on the basis of religion.

Dr Pannikar admits that in its social effects this is a revolutionary idea:

> In a country which has had forty years of history based on separate electorates, communal proportion in all appointments from the meanest to the highest, where a man's preferment depended mainly on his separateness from . . . members of other religions or communities, this is a definite breach with the immediate past.

But he insists that the composite secular state is not 'secularist':

> Secularism in Europe . . . is associated with movements against religious education, against the influence of religious bodies in public life, against the recognition of any special position for religious organizations. The secular state in the West has therefore become identified with an active movement for the elimination of religious influences in the State, and especially in education. This is not the meaning given to the secular state in India. . . . The Indian State by becoming secular has not become irreligious. Its secularism is negative in the sense of not permitting religious considerations to enter into the principles of state action.

And he points to the signal revival of Hinduism, and especially of religious pilgrimage, which not only accompanied the founding of New India, but has been on the increase ever since, in spite of the alienation from all religion of Indians in some circles (not confined to any particular class).

The most significant feature in Indian social life is the combination of what Max Lerner calls the metaphysic of secular promise with the desire for ultimate spiritual liberation. . . . Side by side with [secular progress] one can see a strengthening of religious faith among all classes of people . . . a growth of religious feeling, not dogmatic or sectarian but deeply moved by faith.[1]

It is possible to dismiss this evidence from India, and to predict the arrival there, as elsewhere, of 'religionless man'. But, however short-lived it may prove to be, Independent India proves that it is possible to combine an established secularism with continued, and even revitalized, religious behaviour.

The first *kumbh mela*, a religious festival which takes place once in twelve years at Allahabad, after Independence became almost a demonstration of this revival of faith. More than five million pilgrims gathered on the banks of the Ganges to have a dip in the sacred waters at the Sangam where the Jamuna flows into the Ganges. [There were special trains run, and immense problems for the police of traffic-control.] . . . The frenzy which possessed the pilgrims was indescribable. The President of India and other high dignatories were among the pilgrims.

This was 1948.

[1] Pannikar, op. cit., pp. 244-5.

3

'The Proper Study'

›››◆‹‹‹

We have seen that it is possible to establish a secular society which, once the Queen (theology) has been dethroned, has then allowed, tolerated, and even in rare cases encouraged the assigning of a limited realm to 'non-secular' entities. But may not this in fact be an inconsistent position, required, perhaps, by the Edict of Toleration as a temporary measure to deal with survivals, but bound to disappear in the end?

I. *Behaviour as Mechanism*

It cannot be accidental that of all the Founding Fathers of (what is now known as) Social Science, in Great Britain, America and Europe – Spencer, Durkheim, Comte, Mill, Bentham, Westermarck, Hobhouse, Mannheim, etc. – not one seems to have been 'religious minded', let alone confessedly Christian. And it is, I think, social science which presents most bluntly and forcibly the claims of a secular study. Professor D. Macrae, one of the most sensitive-minded and cultivated sociologists in this country, points to the 'immense liberation' which was felt when it was possible to study the 'history, problems and destiny' of man scientifically, regarding man as a part of nature. Up till 1850 only economics, he says, had an assured status as a 'science of man', though history was beginning to become more scientific; but religious conceptions that man was not comprehensible as a mere part of nature long prevented the emergence of a scientific study of man as social being.[1]

I think we must accept the fact that it was a liberation. Just as the scientific revolution of the 'Renaissance' liberated the study of nature from mythical thinking and a-priori reasoning, to become truly empirical: so to be able at last to include the study of man himself within the secular syllabus gave a sense of freedom for impartial investigation.

Unfortunately, however, it is an easy step from regarding man as part of nature to regarding him as 'merely' part of nature, and then to reducing him to those elements in nature which are most easily measurable. The extreme example of this is to be found in Behaviourism. J. B. Watson, the American psychologist of the twenties, is perhaps a period piece by now. But the 'neo-Behaviourist' school still flourishes. Using mechanistic images of 'conditioning', it compares man's behaviour with that of rats in mazes, or of Pavlov's dogs. One of its exponents, E. C. Tolman, is quite explicit:

I believe that everything important in psychology (except perhaps such matters as the building up of a super-ego, that is everything save such matters as involve society and words) can be investigated in essence through the continued ex-

[1] D. Macrae, *Ideology and Society* (Heinemann, 1961), pp. 122-3.

perimental and theoretical analysis of the determiners of rat behavior at a choice point in a maze.[1]

This is rather like saying that 'everything in *Romeo and Juliet* – except perhaps the hero and heroine, the plot, and the speeches – can be analysed by a study of sexual jealousy among mating otters'. Another psychologist, Clark L. Hull, dismisses the notion of human thinking and willing, and claims that observation of men's behaviour is adequate for understanding his nature:

> We have been quite unable to find any other scientific systems of behaviour which . . . has [*sic*] found consciousness a necessary presupposition. . . . Considering the practically complete failure of all this effort to yield even a small scientific system of adaptive or moral behavior in which consciousness finds a position of logical priority as a postulate, one may, perhaps, be pardoned for entertaining a certain amount of pessimism regarding such an eventuality.[2]

The late Professor Hull did not, however, show much pessimism about the production of his own theories of human behaviour, which were (presumably) consciously elaborated; and the fact that he wrote books to elucidate them implied that he hoped for some modicum of consciousness in potential readers of them. It is difficult to see how intelligent thinkers like these can have been quite so silly.

This 'neo-Behaviourism' is represented in this country by the work of Professor H. J. Eysenck, of the Maudsley

[1] E. C. Tolman, 'The Determinants of Behavior at a Choice Point', *Psych. Rev.* XLV, 1938.

[2] Clark L. Hull, 'Mind, Mechanism and Adoptive Behavior', *Psych. Rev.* XLIV, 1937. These two references are from S. F. Nadel, *The Foundations of Social Anthropology* (Cohen & West, 1951), pp. 61-2.

Hospital, who dismisses psycho-analysis as unscientific mythology, and is only interested in those elements of human behaviour that can be 'factorized' statistically. The results are often interesting, but limited to a very narrow range of human pursuits. No doubt the hope is that with more accurate technique and by amassing a sufficient body of evidence from comparative studies of human behaviour the areas which can be thus scientifically assessed will be widened. I hope we should not wish to discourage the attempt. But there is one simple consideration which vitiates the total claim of such explanations: that human beings not only 'behave' but also have inner beliefs or convictions about what their behaviour is meant to be. When these beliefs or convictions are themselves part of the activity itself, then to analyse the activity abstracted from the beliefs is to fail to analyse it. An American philosopher, Professor John Ladd – who has made a considerable study of social anthropology – has put it this way. The behaviourist may say that a 'belief' or a conviction is simply 'readiness to act', and so can be behaviouristically defined. But suppose (he says) Jones believes that route I is the shortest road to Boston. The behaviourist must say that his belief means the tendency of Jones to take route I when he wants to go to Boston. But this is not enough: for Jones might, mistakenly, take route III, under the misapprehension that it was route I. Then his belief could not be defined as 'Jones' tendency to take route I when he wants to go to Boston' – for in fact he hasn't taken route I at all, but route III. So the behaviourist must say, to be accurate, that Jones' belief that route I is the shortest road to Boston can be defined as 'the tendency of Jones to take route I when he wants to go to Boston, provided, of course, that he believes that the route he is taking is route I'. Thus the behaviourist hasn't managed to get rid of the notion of 'belief': he has to bring it in later. Therefore, says Ladd:

> the more promising way to discover whether a person thought that Route I was the shortest road to Boston would be to ask him, and solely to observe his behavior would be totally misleading.[1]

This philosophical refutation of behaviourism (which seems to me decisive) is confirmed by the increasing tendency of sociologists to take 'subjective' factors into consideration in their analyses of social behaviour and social organization. The assessment, for instance, of the role of 'class' factors in society must, we are realizing, include the computing of answers to questionnaires which ask (among other things), 'What class do you think (or do you feel) you belong to?' Let us assume, for instance, that a major social goal is the product of human 'happiness'; but happiness is a relative concept. As a French writer has remarked, with a cynicism that has truth in it, 'To be happy oneself is not enough: it is necessary that the others shouldn't be'.[2] Here again we see how a purely behaviourist account of human happiness would be unable to make the necessary discriminations: my outward signs of happiness have also to be

[1] John Ladd, *The Structure of a Moral Code* (Harvard, 1957), p. 14.
[2] Macrae, op. cit., pp. 67-8.

interpreted by my secret comparisons of my lot with that of others. And this is all the more true in a competitive, advertisement-sodden world. As Professor Macrae has it:

> We live in a new world where mass-consumption is even more striking than mass-production. . . . In this fundamental social revolution advertising plays a part that is not only big but crucial. Under its impact our social values and the bases of order in society are being destroyed. Advertising is a force which *does not help us to keep up with the Joneses, but which enables the Joneses to keep up with us* [my italics].[1]

Once you regard the study of human behaviour as a form of natural science (which it is), the temptation to employ methods and models from other branches of the natural sciences is almost irresistable. And yet it is fatal. The notion that social science could ever be exactly like the science of mechanics (or of physics or biology), widespread though it is, has been demolished – though its ruins still stand in some places. Perhaps the most unanswerable demolition is contained in a slim volume by a young philosopher, which appeared in 1958 – *The Idea of a Social Science* by Mr Peter Winch.[2] It is a book which is particularly valuable because it starts off from a careful examination of current linguistic philosophy and of the contribution of Wittgenstein. From there it narrows down to the claims of social science. Mr Winch first rejects the behaviourist view, on somewhat similar grounds to those given by Professor Ladd above:

> There is . . . a very simple, but nonetheless cogent,

[1] Macrae, op. cit., p. 70.

[2] Peter Winch, *The Idea of a Social Science* (Routledge, 1958).

argument against the physiological interpretation of motive. To discover the motives of a puzzling action *is* to increase our understanding of that action. . . . But this is something we in fact discover without any significant knowledge about people's physiological states.[1]

In other words, what must appear to the behaviourist one and the same action (e.g., *A* giving a parcel to *B*) may in fact be a whole variety of actions, according to the motives involved. (The parcel may be a thank-offering; it may be a time-bomb; it may be an apparently generous gift which in fact is designed to augment the pride, and so the power, of the giver . . . and so on. The possibilities are almost infinite, but totally ignored by the behaviourist account.) But what about J. S. Mill's more modest claim: that to understand a social institution is to observe regularities in the behaviour of its participants, as one examines (say) the tides, or nest-building, and then to express these regularities in generalizations? So far as it goes, this sounds all right. But, says Mr Winch, the difficulty is that

Whereas in the case of the natural scientist we have to deal with only one set of rules, namely those governing the scientists' investigations itself, here *what the sociologist is studying*, as well as his study of it, is a human activity and is therefore carried on according to rules.

He gives as an example the parable of the Pharisee and the Publican (Luke 18.9). Both men were in the same temple, both performing a similar function (worshipping). Was the Pharisee then doing the same kind of thing as the Publican? Obviously not. But to say

[1] Winch, op. cit., p. 78.

'obviously not' one must first know what is involved in the idea of prayer. And that is a religious, not a sociological question. And so

> A historian or sociologist of religion must himself have some religious feeling if he is to make sense of the religious movement he is studying and understand the considerations which govern the lives of its participants.[1]

And this goes for other topics too. A historian of art must have some aesthetic sense if he is to understand the problems confronting the artists of his period – otherwise he will leave out of account precisely what makes it a history of *art*, rather than a puzzled account of certain strange gestures made by a class of eccentric humans. If, says Winch, you are going to compare the social student to an engineer, then you'll do better

> to compare him to an apprentice engineer who is studying what engineering . . . is all about. His understanding of social phenomena is more like the engineer's understanding of his colleague's activity than it is like the engineer's understanding of the mechanical systems which he studies.

To understand human behaviour is more like learning a language than like observing statistical regularities, or even being able to predict from these regularities what sort of behaviour will most probably be met with in the future. Thus, it would be possible without knowing a word of Chinese to study Chinese ideograms, to count the frequency with which certain of them occur in sentences, and thus to calculate the probability of such and such an ideogram occurring so many times in future

[1] Winch, op. cit., p. 88.

sentences. But this would tell us nothing about the meaning, or the importance of that particular ideogram in a phrase. Indeed, like the letter 'and' in English, its very frequency might point to its *un*importance. And so the social scientist must in the last resort operate like the historian. For historical explanation

is like applying one's knowledge of a language in order to understand a conversation rather than like applying one's knowledge of the laws of mechanics to understand the workings of a watch.[1]

II. *Society as Function*

This dispute between the quasi-mechanistic and the humanistic notions of social science has appeared again recently in the – more subtle – controversy between the 'historical' and the 'anti-historical' schools of social anthropology today. The latter, commonly known as the 'functionalist' view, was expounded by such influential anthropologists as Malinowski and Radcliffe-Brown. The last-named, especially, believed that you could understand social phenomena best by studying their social functions. This means, of course, that you deliberately refuse to pass value-judgements on these phenomena.

A savage tribe practising polygamy, cannibalism, and sorcery can possibly show a higher degree of functional unity or consistency than (say) the United States of 1935. This objective judgement, for such it must be if it is to be scientific, is something very different from any judgement as to which of the two social systems is the better.[2]

[1] Winch, op. cit., p. 133.

[2] A. R. Radcliffe-Brown, *Structure in Function and Primitive Society* (Cohen & West, 1952), p. 183, note.

Radcliffe-Brown had to admit that there may be some rites that have no apparent social function at all (e.g., the taboo against spilling salt in our own society). But he claimed that to study rites as 'symbolic expressions' and to try to discover their social functions has been the most rewarding, because the method that is least subjective and prejudiced. And he claimed that it is useful to employ both biological and physiological analogies when speaking of societies. Every kind of social phenomenon, he says – morals, law, etiquette, religion, government and education – is part of 'the complex mechanism by which a social structure exists and persists'.[1]

The weakness of this view is that it ignores history. A 'mechanism' has no history. Professor Macrae, criticizing this view, says that it may derive from Burke in the eighteenth century:

> Societies are seamless, consistent and logical. Historical questions cannot therefore expect to yield answers of much explanatory value.[2]

But how, in that case, could there ever be any 'endogenous social change' within such a static structure? And so Professor E. E. Evans-Pritchard, the leader of the opposite, 'historical' school of social anthropology protests that social facts and social structures are not static entities but develop through time and cannot be understood apart from their history. The view that social systems are 'natural systems' and so reducible to sociological laws, he says 'seems to me to be doctrinaire positivism at its worst'. He challenges those who support

[1] Radcliffe-Brown, op. cit., pp. 196ff. [2] Macrae, op. cit., pp. 43-5.

this view to produce sociological laws similar to those laws formulated by natural scientists:

> Up to the present nothing even remotely resembling what are called laws in the natural sciences has been adduced – only rather naïve deterministic, teleological and pragmatic assertions. The generalizations which have been attempted have been . . . so vague and general as to be of little use, and . . . tautologies and platitudes on the level of common sense deduction.[1]

No doubt one of the reasons for the opposition to Professor Evans-Pritchard and the 'historical' school may be a suspicion that it might turn into a kind of 'metaphysics of history' (what might be called an Anthropological Toynbee-itis), and that Professor Evans-Pritchard, instead of sharpening the social anthropologists' tools, may be depriving them of the exactitude of a natural science and offering instead the vague descriptions of social history. Perhaps Professor Macrae's comment is the most judicious:

> As a sociologist I think functionalism a form or error – though not all error . . . and fruitful error. [It is useful in the field, but it] may have tempted some workers to stress social unity and ignore schism in an unrealistic fashion. Yet it is hard to think of a better tool for research among primitive and peasant people without documentation to whom quantitative techniques cannot be applied.[2]

These disputes may seem both remote and technical; but they reveal interestingly the extent to which metaphors and models, used (often unthinkingly) by

[1] E. E. Evans-Pritchard, *Social Anthropology* (Cohen & West, 1951), p. 57.
[2] Macrae, ibid.

students of society, can influence their interpretations or explanations of what they are observing.

III. *Society as Organism*

One of the most powerfully influential metaphors for society is that of 'organism'. Organisms grow, change, are subject to mutation, and even to sudden, violent modifications from within as well as without. They have a history, and a direction. Auguste Comte long ago saw a pattern of human development which has been taken over, often quite uncritically, by thinkers ever since. The pattern was of three Stages of Man – Theological, Metaphysical and Positive. Once you accept that pattern you will tend to read it backwards into the history of any social phenomenon you are investigating.

It is true that Comte did not think of any stage as wholly abandoned: each one is taken up into the stage that supersedes it. Thus, he had no desire to abolish the 'religious sense' in man. Indeed, to comfort those who felt a sense of loss with the theological and the metaphysical snatched away from them, he offered a Religion of Humanity, with its Creed, its Liturgy, its Hierarchy and its Hagiology. The cult of 'Sociolatry', as Comte called it, is expressed and symbolized, and the emotional attitude necessary for it is stimulated, by the private and public worship of the Religion of Humanity. Private worship is to be based on 'the adoration of the best types we can find to personify humanity': e.g., on the worship of Woman as the domestic goddess. There are the Guardian Angels, *sc.* mother = veneration, wife = attachment and daughter = kindness. In effect, we are to adore our family circle; and if our family happens to contain 'bad elements', then we must 'recreate it subjectively'. (On hearing this, the Lady in the *Positive Catechism*, who is being instructed in the Faith, says 'These remarks complete the subject'.) Private prayers are said on waking, at midday, and on retiring to rest – prayer = invoking the 'Angels'. There are nine 'Social Sacraments' – Presentation, Initiation, Admission, Destination, Marriage, Maturity, Retirement, Transformation (a form of extreme unction but without what Comte calls the loneliness of 'the Catholics' horrible ceremony') and Incorporation (= Canonization, seven years after death). Public Worship is based on the new Positive Calendar, in which Humanity (symbolized by mother and child) is adored in a series of four-week festivals, divided into two kinds – Static and Dynamic Festivals – for which the Arts are called in to give the utmost ritual grandeur to the celebration of social order and progress. And the *Catechism* ends with the unambiguous claim that:

> Now Humanity definitively occupies the place of God; but . . . she does not forget the services which the idea of God provisionally rendered.[1]

This comic spectacle of Comte creating a synthetic secular religion may lead us to overlook the important fact that, while the attempt to redirect the 'religious' emotions into positivist channels clearly failed, the general picture of the three Stages of Man remained

[1] Cited in B. Willey, *Nineteenth-Century Studies* (Chatto, 1949), pp. 200f.

enormously influential as a way of interpreting human history. One suspects that even some Christian thinkers who have rather loosely and uncritically employed the late Dietrich Bonhoeffer's phrase about modern man 'come of age' are really victims of Comte's pervasive influence.

But there is a strange, and not often noticed, confusion at the base of this picture. Man evolves, we are told, through these three stages, like the evolution of an organism. But the general direction of evolution seems to have been away from inanimate, through sub-animate, to animate and finally to intelligent beings; whereas the last stage of the Comtean process, the 'positive-scientific', is described in mechanistic language. Thus there is talk today in cybernetic circles about the 'intelligence' of the computer. If a computer can now be programmed to do more complex operations of memory, selection and prediction than the human brain can compass, must we not say that the computer will one day be 'more intelligent' than man? And if you reply that even the best computer can only imitate, derivatively, the activity of man (who after all has to do the 'programming'), the cyberneticist will retort, 'On the contrary: the human brain can now be shown to be making rather slow and feeble attempts at imitating the superior mathematical ability of the computer.' In that case, we have to add a fourth stage to Comte's three 'Stages of Man': beyond the theological, the metaphysical and the positive-scientific is the cybernetic – which might be called the 'post-animate stage' of evolution.

There are, of course, philosophical difficulties about this position, very similar to those which face the behaviourist discussed in the first section. Professor D. M. Mackay, especially, has shown the inadequacy of the popular cyberneticist view in two respects. First, human activity when it is free is also conscious of itself as free. Suppose I am a physicist and a neurologist. Then I can describe the operations of a mechanical 'brain' (call it 'Rex'). I can then X-ray your skull, apply cathodes, make an EEG of its operations, etc.; and so describe the operations of your brain. The two descriptions, of Rex's 'brain' and yours, look exactly on the same level. But they aren't. For if I tell you what I am describing, your brain will immediately react to my description and behave differently. ('One of the best ways of making an angry man more angry,' says MacKay, 'is by telling him he is getting angry.') In other words, man is 'committed' to his thought and his behaviour in a way that no computer however complex can ever be. And secondly, MacKay points to the uniqueness of inter-personal relations. If, in my psychological approach to you I start trying to treat you as if you were a mere machine (indeed, as a computer) – which is what all forms of exploitation, tyranny, etc., are doing – then I shall alter your attitude to me. I may even succeed in turning you into a computer by prolonged conditioning; but you will not then be any longer the real 'you'.[1]

[1] D. M. MacKay, 'On the Logical Indeterminacy of a Free Choice', *Mind* NS LXIX, No. 273, Jan., 1960, and cf. MacKay, 'The Use of Behavioural Language to refer to Mechanical Processes', *Brit. Journal for Phil. of Science* XII, No. 50, Aug., 1962, pp. 89ff.,

All this was foreseen long ago in a book which has, I think, been unduly neglected: Professor John Macmurray's *The Boundaries of Science* (1939). He traces the history of the extension of the natural sciences. The physical sciences are of course the most exact. When you reach economics you reach a border-line case: it is a 'psychological science', but it must assume that there are certain objective economic laws, though these are only formulations from human habits of behaviour. It is significant, he says, that in the early days sociology preferred to study primitive society, because it is relatively easy to stand outside that and to survey it scientifically, i.e., treating society as ruled by observable laws. But what happens when we try to understand our own society? As sociologists we must believe that our society too operates by observable, i.e. unconscious laws. Yet society has produced us (sociologists) who have chosen to do this particular type of study. And Macmurray points to the paradox that sociology arose largely from man's desire to control and free society from its conservative inhibitions, and thus with a desire to control and change society[1]: and yet as a science it must assume that social behaviour is independent of human will and intention. So, if scientific investigations are to cover the whole field of human behaviour, the scientist 'must assume that there is no part of his behaviour (even the

and 'Mentality in Machines', *Proc. Arist. Soc. Suppl.* 1952, 26, pp. 61-86.

[1] It is interesting that Professor D. Macrae, who has probably not read Macmurray's book, says, 'If you scratch a sociologist you will find a moralist or a preacher' (op. cit., p. 78).

activity of observing the behaviour) which is really his behaviour'. The same paradox faces the psychologist. The psychologist's behaviour in producing psychology must, on this theory, be represented as a set of processes which happen according to objective laws. But then

> The psychologist's account of psychology, if it is scientific, must exclude the possibility of considering it either true or false. His theory must be a theory such that, if it is true, it cannot be true.[1]

Macmurray is careful to insist that these paradoxes do not mean that social science or psychology are illegitimate activities, nor that they are bogus sciences. Science in practice justifies itself in both these fields. But the paradoxes do point to the limitations in their application – hence the title of his book, the 'Boundaries of Science'. And I think it ought to be emphasized that, though we may think some of the theoretical and speculative conclusions of scientists in these fields unwarranted, their scientific motivation has been a laudable desire for exactitude, an unwillingness to generalize beyond the evidence, and therefore basically an attitude of humility.

IV. *Evolution Up or Down?*

In the last section we started from the metaphor of 'organism' as applied to society. We shall see in the next chapter that 'evolution' is a tricky concept to use of man's ethical behaviour. But we must first look at its implications for the understanding of social processes.

In the first place, there are very diverse ways of inter-

[1] J. Macmurray, *The Boundaries of Science* (Faber, 1939), p. 126.

preting an 'evolutionary sociology'. Darwin notoriously believed that the fact of evolution was a guarantee of, and therefore a spur to progress. An anti-evolutionary view would be that of a primitive innocence, a paradise, from which men fell. But said Darwin:

to believe that man was aboriginally civilized and then suffered utter degradation . . . is to take a pitiably low view of human nature.

And he believed it a truer view that progress has been more general than retrogression; that

man has risen, though by slow and interrupted steps, from a lowly condition to the highest standard as yet attained by him in knowledge, morals and religion.[1]

In other words, progress and evolution are mutually implicated. But this is not the only way of reading evolution. T. H. Huxley believed that man's only hope of development, perhaps of survival, was for him to strive 'against' the evolutionary process, against the 'down-pull' of natural forces. On the other hand, scientists like Julian Huxley, J. B. S. Haldane or the late Père Teilhard de Chardin, believe that in man we meet 'evolution conscious of itself'; that the human rational and personal processes are the only possible, and the necessary, further stages of an evolution that has come to a dead-end (through over-specialization and consequent atrophy or elephantiasis) in other species.

On the other hand, there have been evolutionary theorists (Dr S. B. Leakey is one, and we shall see in the last chapter Professor Muller, the zoologist, suggesting

[1] C. Darwin, *The Descent of Man* (Murray, 1901), p. 224.

something similar) who have hinted that human evolution itself may be showing signs of this dead-endedness. The suggestion is that so long as man, like other animals, lived in a primitive and predatory state, wars between the hordes, famine and disease kept his population at a proper ecological level, that is, balanced with his environment. But since man has learned kindness and cooperation, since his scientific development has enabled him to reduce the death-rate, while his virility still maintains the birth-rate, he has been slowly (and is now swiftly) approaching his self-extinction through over-population.

Another interpretation of evolution, in its crude Darwinian terms as 'survival of the fittest', has been as an invitation or a command to racial exclusiveness or class intolerance. This has taken two opposite forms. The German historian, Otto Ammon, analysed human history in Darwinian terms, using especially the criteria of physical anthropology, and came to optimistic conclusions: it is the upper classes who prove taller and more long-headed, and therefore are obviously more fitted for survival:

> Only and exclusively the type of man who has developed in the north of Europe with its inclement climate under the influence of hunting, of war and of knightly exercises offers those endowments which constitute the glories of the Aryan race, namely strength, energy, bravery, self-appreciation, love of truth, sympathy for the weak and genuine humanity.[1]

[1] O. Ammon, *Die Gesellschaftsordnung und ihr natürlichen Grundlagen* (Jena, 1895): cited in W. Stark, 'Natural and Social Selection' in M. Banton (ed.), *Darwinism and the Study of Society* (Tavistock Publ., 1961), p. 51.

On the other hand another historian, Georges Vascher de Lapouge, writing at the same time, draws the opposite, pessimistic conclusions from precisely the same type of evidence. He sees social selection as invariably bringing out the worst: it is the poor who thrive, the genetically least fit who survive. And the result will be the inevitable and complete degeneration of the human race. He echoes the warnings of Comte de Gobineau, who wrote in similar vein before him.

> Racial mixture is the most obvious, the most certain, and the most enduring effect of the great societies. . . . Once it has come about, the age of uniformity will begin. . . . All men will resemble each other . . . and this general level will bring the most revolting humiliation. The nations, or rather, the human herds, weighed down by a dismal somnolence, will then lead to a torpid existence, like the ruminating buffaloes in the stagnant mires of the Pontine marshes. . . . [In the end] the globe, become silent, will continue to describe its impassive circles in space – but without us.

For race-mixture will have ended in race-extinction.[1]

This sort of nonsense will seem not worth attention. And yet, the practical effect of Darwinian notions upon nineteenth-century *laissez-faire* economics, and therefore upon an expanding capitalism, can hardly be exaggerated. And even today one hears echoes of this deification of evolutionary processes in propaganda for the 'competitive society'. Readers of William Whyte's *The Organization Man* will remember the President of the 'Vick School of Applied Merchandising', who

[1] Joseph Arthur Comte de Gobineau, *Essai sur l'Inégalité des Races Humaines* (Paris, 1855) IV, p. 346: cited in Stark, op. cit., p. 55.

had strong views on the necessity of holding to the old American virtues [and warned his pupils emphatically against] letting sentimentality obscure fundamentals. Business was the survival of the fittest, he indicated, and we would soon learn the fact.[1]

It becomes clear, then, that 'evolution' is not an easy concept, and that when applied to human society it can be given a variety of interpretations. This is not surprising, for a similar variety of interpretations is given of non-human, or pre-human evolution. Two contemporary examples of the optimistic versus the pessimistic interpretations can be found in the works of Teilhard de Chardin and of the French biologist, Jean Rostand. Teilhard began his *Le Phénomène humain* before nuclear fission was thought possible; he concluded it after Hiroshima; and yet he altered not one word of the earlier version which expressed an obstinate faith that man's future is *guaranteed* to him by the evolutionary process of which he is both the crown and the meaning, and therefore that gloomy prognostications about man's ability to commit telluric suicide (through nuclear war or whatever) must be discounted if evolution is true. By contrast, Jean Rostand sees no single direction of evolution.

The picture presented to us of life's evolution astounds us by its high talents. . . and disconcerts us by the use to which they are put. Incoherent, improvident, wasteful and tumultuous, as heedless of failure as of success; creating at random in every style and direction; prodigal in discarding the new; launching one species against another; creating both har-

[1] W. Whyte, *The Organization Man* (Cape, 1957), p. 114.

mony and the grotesque; unmindful of what is necessary but meticulous in what is superfluous, and creating impartially that which will survive through the ages, that which will degenerate and that which will continue to progress.[1]

Teilhard welcomed all new discovery – space travel, nuclear fission, even the possible synthetic creation of 'life'. Rostand, the agnostic, was sometimes more hesitant about scientific development:

I must admit that there are moments when I wonder whether man will always be able to accept the new picture of himself which science offers him, whether he will go on indefinitely adapting himself to his increasing knowledge, whether he will be able to assimilate all his inventions without endangering his emotional balance. It may well be that the progress of biology will lead us along paths too remote from what is human and where our deepest needs are too often thwarted. May it not be that by mishandling nature, we are going to create a climate for men in which they will not be able to breathe? Just as there are limits to radioactivity beyond which we must not go, so too, in the spiritual and moral order, there are perhaps mysterious frontiers which must not be crossed if we are not to bring the human animal to a state of confusion and solitude.[2]

V. *Culture as Transmission*

But if so many different interpretations of evolution can be given, can we really say that the use of metaphors of 'organism' for human society is helpful – is it not more misleading than illuminating? Some experts think

[1] Jean Rostand, *A Biologist's View* (Heinemann, 1956), pp. 25f.

[2] Rostand, 'Pour une Morale biologique' in *Demain*, 30 Oct., 1957: cited in S. de Lestapis, *Family Planning and Modern Problems* (Burns & Oates, 1961), p. 221.

so. An eminent zoologist, Mr J. Maynard Smith, is clear that a useful theory of history cannot be constructed, starting from evolution theory, and attempting to find historical parallels to the various entities and processes involved. 'Evolution', he says, 'would be more like history if Lamarckian inheritance were true.'[1]

Most biologists today reject 'Lamarckian' theories of the inheritance of acquired characteristics; for (apart from the rather subtle discussion of 'epigenetic systems', and their mimicking of 'Lamarckian processes', by Professor C. H. Waddington and others) it is generally held that only genetic inheritance is possible – i.e., what is not 'carried by' the genes cannot be passed on. But it is obvious that one of the characteristics of human society is that its inheritance is not merely genetic. The passing on of genes for red-hairedness, or long-nosedness, is less significant for human society than the passing on of acquired skills, new knowledge, cultural habits, and, above all, language-systems. Doesn't it look, indeed, as if human development (as T. H. Huxley held) is in the opposite direction from that of cosmic evolution?

Time on the scale of evolution has an arrow which, in some sense, points towards higher order. But in dead nature, the arrow of time points the other way. The atoms want always to move towards a state of lower order, towards an even mixture which will be undifferentiated and featureless. For dead nature, time is a running-down movement towards more probable, that is, more unordered states. By contrast, life is a constant resistance to this running-down of time, a

[1] J. Maynard Smith, 'Evolution and History' in M. Banton (ed.), *Darwinism*, p. 114.

constant choice, a constant recreation of miraculously improbable states of order.[1]

But there is surely a similar tension between the 'down-pull' and the 'up-pull', within human social life itself. In so far as men are controlled, even overwhelmed by 'material' factors (economic, nutritive, etc.), their organization tends towards a 'death-state'; in so far as they combat this process and exercise control over their environment, society progresses. This is not, therefore, out of line with evolution – especially biological evolution. And if we think of the four time-scales of evolution, expounded by Professor Waddington, we shall find that one in particular (the third) is highly appropriate to man. The four scales are: first, the 'hour-to-hour, or minute-to-minute' operations of living things – changes which can be observed under a microscope; then the longer process, occurring in a period of time comparable to a life-time, by which the egg grows into the adult, then to old age, and then death. Then there is the third scale, the length of several life-times, which is needed to be able to measure heredity (characteristics of organisms passed on from parent to offspring): one generation is not enough to be significant for this. And finally comes the scale of hundreds of generations, the slow processes of evolution 'by which the character of the individuals in a given population gradually changes and the population may become split up into two or more different species.'[2]

This third time-scale provides the closest analogies

[1] J. Bronowsky's Introduction to M. Banton (ed.), *Darwinism*, p. xx.
[2] C. H. Waddington, *The Nature of Life* (Allen & Unwin, 1961), p. 27.

between biological and human-social evolution: the time, that is, taken for processes of heredity to be detectable – though, as we have said, in human societies it is cultural heredity that is more important than physical. The point is that the analogy of evolution *is* illuminating here, when properly discriminated. And note, too, that there can be the same strange and unpredictable variations in speed, in length of time for hereditary mutations to 'register', both in biology and in sociology. Just as there can be sudden genetic 'spurts', so there can be rapid cultural adaptations. Indeed, one anthropologist has argued that sometimes rapid adaptations are more effective. Dr Margaret Mead has done a close study of one such rapid change, among the Manus people on an island off New Guinea. She points out that, from her earlier experience with the same people twenty-five years earlier (1928-9), she and others would have predicted a slow change, with the coming of Western influences. But in fact when she went back in 1953-4, she discovered that the Westernization had been speedy and wholesale. How could this be? She answers:

> Because of the unpredictable in human life. . . . In real-life situations we always have to come to terms with sequences of events which are outside the limited little set of conditions within which we have learned to predict. So the bridge-builder constructing a bridge in New Guinea may understand perfectly the nature of the steel . . . and still his bridge may fail to materialize because his crew died of an epidemic of Japanese River-fever, or . . . an earthquake may come and shatter his cement posts.[1]

[1] Margaret Mead, *New Lives for Old* (Gollancz, 1956), pp. 103f.

But her conclusion is that in this case at least this, though unexpected, proved to be the best way of adaptation.

Rapid change is not only possible, but may actually be very desirable – that instead of advocating slow partial changes, we should advocate that a people who choose to practise a new technology or enter into drastically new kinds of economic relationships will do this more easily if they live in different houses, wear different clothes, and eat different, or differently cooked, food. . . . [Whereas] partial change – [like] installing new kinds of office furniture in out-of-date reconverted dwelling houses – can be seen not as a bridge between old and new, but rather as the condition within which discordant and discrepant institutions and practices develop and proliferate – with corresponding discrepancies and discordances in the lives of those who live within them.[1]

It is to studies like Margaret Mead's that Professor Waddington appeals when he justifies using evolutionary language to describe social processes. And we may take one rather different area, in which interesting studies have been made recently, to illustrate the validity of the biological analogy: politics! The American social historian, Seymour Martin Lipset, in an examination of 'the sociology of politics', points out that a democratic system has to operate in a paradoxical way. It has to retain sufficient 'play', sufficient room for conflict or cleavage, for there to be genuine struggle over ruling positions, genuine freedom for controversy and competition; and yet, of course, it must not become sheerly anarchic, it must retain sufficient 'consensus' of the general public for it to continue as a democracy. How can these two, apparently contradictory, forces (what he

[1] Mead, op. cit., pp. 450f.

calls 'cleavage' and 'consensus') be maintained simultaneously? The answer seems to be that there is a sort of 'self-righting' process within societies which (like a thermostat control) as it were switches off consent when there isn't adequate cleavage, or when cleavage becomes too strong switches on consent again. And Lipset shows, from both British and American studies of elections, that something like this can be pointed to in action. When a democratic system is cohesive and stable, all parts of the population will tend to react in the same direction to major stimuli. That is,

> if conditions facilitate the growth of leftist opinion, the socialists will gain votes among both the well-to-do and the workers, though they will remain relatively weaker in the upper strata. In the same way, during a period of right-wing ascendancy conservative votes will increase among the poorer group.

But conversely, if we find a political tendency growing only among groups to whom it primarily appeals – if the left-wing gains among workers and the right-wing among the 'upper' classes – then we have an unstable, low-consent, democracy.[1]

Thus the sociologist is able, in a modest way, to produce some statistical evidence that societies behave like organisms. In the biology of evolutionary change there is what is known technically as 'genetic homeostasis' – a form of self-righting balance. Primary or 'homeostatic' needs are such things as hunger, the maintainance of a particular skin temperature, etc., in the

[1] S. M. Lipset, *Political Man* (Heinemann, 1960), p. 33.

animal. Most animals, and mammals certainly, also develop certain 'non-homeostatic' needs – in infants, such activities as sucking, crying, clinging and smiling can best be explained in this way. These are subsidiary needs, and yet can still be seen as contingent parts of evolutionary development.[1] Perhaps these 'non-homeostatic needs' find their analogies in man's political behaviour.

But even granted that the use of evolutionary or organic language, applied to human societies, can be justified (some might say, with a little ingenuity), is it worth it? Does it really help? Should we be any the worse without it? It is, after all, impossible for man wholly to disinfect his interpretations of anthropomorphism; and since man is (among other things) essentially a 'myth-making' or 'dramatizing' animal, his reading of the evolutionary process can easily merge from cold semi-statistical statement into dramatic portrayal. He can see the course of nature as farce, as drawing-room comedy, as tragedy, or as grand-guignol. (We have seen Teilhard de Chardin and Jean Rostand composing their diametrically opposite types of drama out of its material.) Surely this is not 'science'?

And here, precisely, I believe is the value of the evolutionary metaphors. What is in common to these varied views and dramatizations is at least the conviction that the human animal cannot be isolated from the biological tree; and more, the excitement, the *élan*, the illumination – though accompanied by the anxiety and

[1] S. A. Barnett, 'Communication in Animal and Human Societies' in M. Banton (ed.), *Darwinism*, pp. 146f.

even the terror – that comes from finding that your topic is wider than you thought. It is intriguing to discover that the cottage you often stay in, on holiday, has a corner made of stones taken from some Saxon ruin. It is wonderfully enlightening to discover by chance reading that the novel you have just written is based, quite unknown to you, on a theme which can be discovered (say) in an old Norse poem, or among the traditions of the Arapesh. And so, to be able to place man's social, political, even individual behaviour against a background of the long development of the planet is a salutary, humbling exercise. We saw in chapter two that the old theological 'Argument from Design' has had largely to be abandoned. But as a contemporary psychologist (Miss M. Brierley) has said:

> It was not too difficult for the rationalists to show that many religious beliefs and dogmas were not corroborated by the findings of natural science. In the first flush of pride in the achievements of human reason it never occurred to them that they were dealing only with the superficial manifestations of profound needs which religion had at least appeased. We know more now about the intricate organization of the psyche. Although the argument from design does not convince us of the objective existence of God, it does induce in us a more becoming intellectual humility.[1]

The same kind of humility is no doubt induced by the thought of man's insignificance against the background of modern cosmological theories – and either the 'steady-state' or the 'big bang' theories will serve equally here. It used to be said that this was one effect of the Copernican

[1] M. Brierley, *Trends in Psychoanalysis* (Hogarth, 1951), p. 100.

revolution: that to remove the earth from its geocentric position was to humble man. But, as Professor A. O. Lovejoy pointed out some years ago, the medieval geocentric view did not put man at the centre of the universe:

> It has often been said that the older picture of the world in space was peculiarly fitted to give man a high sense of his own importance and dignity. . . . Man occupied, we are told, the central place in the universe, and round the planet of his habitation all the vast, unpeopled spheres obsequiously rolled. But the actual tendency of the geocentric system was, for the medieval mind, precisely the opposite. For the centre of the world was not a position of honour; it was rather the place farthest removed from the Empyrean, the bottom of the creation, to which its dregs and baser elements sank. The actual centre, indeed, was Hell; in the spatial sense the medieval world was literally diabolocentric.[1]

Perhaps the thought of man in the cosmos is one which it is difficult to remain aware of for very long at a time – it makes for vertigo more often than for humility. But awareness of man's place in the evolutionary scheme is something we can be reminded of every time we suffer from a virus infection; and whenever we are disheartened by man's slow growth in moral understanding or sensitivity, we can, perhaps, find some comfort in reflection on geological time-scales. Indeed, it could be said that the biologists from time to time teach us the spiritual lesson of the psalmist who said, not in a moment of pessimism or cynicism, but of realism, that

'*I am a worm, and no man*'.

[1] A. O. Lovejoy, *The Great Chain of Being* (Harvard, 1936), pp. 101f.

4

The Moral Animal

›››◆‹‹‹

I. *Morals and Religion*

WE saw in the last chapter that there are secular sociologists and biologists who claim that to place man in an evolutionary context is to gain illumination upon the nature and functioning of his societies. And we have allowed that at least this method leads to a proper reverence for the larger processes in which man is, so to speak, graciously permitted to play his part.

On the other hand, it has honestly to be admitted that the practical results of this new understanding are meagre; that the programmes for man's behaviour, or the predictions about the future shape of his social relationships, which can be deduced from a knowledge of man's evolutionary past, are very limited. It is surely significant that the most valuable and fruitful recommendations which the social scientists can offer are, on the whole, those which have the most remote resemblance to the biological or organic analogies which some of them are still in the habit of using when describing social entities.

At this point Christian apologists are wont to jump in with glee, and say 'Of course: what do you expect? Can you not see that the essential difference between human societies and other organisms lies in man's moral-religious nature? Man alone in the animal kingdom is an ethical being; and there have never been ethics without religion.'

This position has been backed by formidable arguments. So learned a cultural historian as Mr Christopher Dawson has claimed categorically that:

> Everywhere the moral law is based ultimately on religious sanctions. . . . The rules by which the life of a primitive community is governed are all sacred rules enforced by religious sanctions.[1]

Or, if Mr Dawson as a Roman Catholic be thought a biased witness, there is Professor Karl Popper: 'Historically, all ethics undoubtedly begins with religion.'[2]

However, this view has been challenged: notably by Professor A. Macbeath, in his Gifford Lectures for 1952, in which he studied in some detail four 'primitive' cultures and argued on the basis of the available evidence that in none of these four was the whole of morality based on supernatural notions. The Crow Indians, for instance: though their military operations were indeed inspired by a religious revelation, the contents of their supernatural visions were 'socially or culturally determined'.[3] With the Trobriand Islanders 'few of their rules of conduct' (according to Malinowski) 'have super-

[1] C. Dawson, *Religion and Culture* (Sheed & Ward, 1947), p. 155.

[2] K. Popper, *The Open Society and its Enemies* (Routledge, 1945) I, p. 55.

[3] A. Macbeath, *Experiments in Living* (Macmillan, 1952), p. 234.

natural sanctions'.[1] Of the Australian aborigines it seems to be true that they

> have no idea whatever of the existence of any supreme being who is pleased if they follow a certain line of what we call moral conduct and displeased if they do not.[2]

And perhaps the clearest example of all is the Tonga people (a Bantu tribe of South Africa), who made a distinction between 'magico-moral' rules, which concern ritual relationships, and 'socio-moral' rules which have no supernatural sanction. Junod, the great student of the Tonga, said:

> Bantu religion is a non-moral religion, by which I do not mean that it is immoral . . . but that it has no, or at least very little, connection with the moral conduct of the individual. It has no moral prescriptions except those that ensure the hierarchical order in the family. It neither promises rewards nor threatens punishment after death. . . . The ancestor-gods are non-moral. If the great fault of Bantu religion is that it is non-moral, that of Bantu morality is that it is non-religious. No supreme legislator has ordained it. Hence the want of the idea of the absolute in the dictates of the Bantu conscience. Nevertheless the rudiments of morality are present in the Tonga conscience, the feeling of duty, the sense of right and wrong. These are independent of the essentially self-interested ideas of taboo.[3]

To these examples cited by Professor Macbeath we could add another not mentioned by him: the Navaho Indians. The expert on their customs, Fr Bernard Haile,

[1] Macbeath, op. cit., pp. 148f.

[2] Ibid., p. 211, quoting Spencer and Gillen, *Northern Tribes of Central Australia*, p. 491.

[3] Ibid., pp. 186-8, quoting Junod, *The Life of a S. African Tribe* II, pp. 427f., 582-3.

has explained that Navaho theology seems to be limited to certain ritual ceremonies (the Indians called them 'Sings'); and their religious system

> is not concerned with the ethics of an action, except in so far as we equate ethics with transgressions of tabus and restrictions. . . . Such basic concepts as conscience, morality, law and a host of other concepts do not enter Navaho ideology.

And elsewhere the same authority concludes that 'In the Navaho system there is no supreme law-giver or pantheon of lawgivers concerned with the morals of humans and supernaturals'.[1]

This looks decisive. But there are difficulties here. For Professor Radcliffe-Brown, who as we saw in the last chapter was the great exponent of the 'functionalist' approach to social anthropology, and who would therefore have no predispositions in favour of a case argued by (say) Mr Christopher Dawson, criticizes those who maintain that in many primitive societies 'morals' and 'religion' were separate notions. He suggests that this often means merely that 'in the "lower races" the religion is not associated with the kind of morality which exists in contemporary Western societies'. He adduces evidence from the very sources drawn upon by (e.g.) Professor Macbeath – the Australian aborigines and the Trobriand Islands' societies – tending to show that there *is* some connection between their notions of

[1] J. Ladd, *The Structure of a Moral Code*, pp. 314, 268, quoting B. Haile, *Annali Lateranensi* 1945, VII, pp. 84, 94; and *The Americas* (1950) VII, No. 1, p. 70.

moral behaviour and their notions of religion. He prefers to state the complex relationship in a more subtle, less loaded way – indeed, in terms of 'function':

> Law, morality and religion are three ways of controlling human conduct which in different types of society supplement one another, and are combined in different ways. For the law there are legal sanctions, for morality there are the sanctions of public opinion and of conscience, for religion there are religious sanctions. And one deed may come under two or three.[1]

The dispute seems partly a verbal one: what should we count as a 'religious' sanction? If '*re-ligio*' has any connection with its most obvious etymology, can there be total dissociation between a 'binding' rule and some – however inchoate – 'religious' concepts? But the dispute at least makes clear that Christian apologists should beware of making too simple and direct claims for a necessary connection between theology and morals. The secularist view, that man as ethical being can, at least in certain civilizations, be fully described without recourse to any 'supernatural' reference, though it must be regarded as unproven, cannot be dismissed out of hand.

II. *Evolutionary Ethics*

But what of the moral sense itself, quite apart from its possible religious reference? Can a 'naturalistic' account of that be given? For certainly one of the most characteristic qualities of man is his moral sense: if, then an evolutionary view of man can adequately account

[1] Radcliffe-Brown, *Structure and Function*, p. 172.

for that moral sense, this will be a powerful reason in favour of employing the organic, biological types of analogy for human societies.

The study of 'evolutionary ethics' has been a preoccupation of many sociologically-minded biologists of recent years. There is no space to look at all these studies, but it is worth examining the best of them, contained in the relevant work of Professor C. H. Waddington.

Waddington's early attempt in this mode was, as a matter of fact, unhappy. In the little volume, *Science and Ethics* (1942), he offered an account of evolutionary ethics which was subjected to severe criticisms both by psychologists and by philosophers. One passage in the controversy strikingly revealed the inadequacy of evolutionary concepts to explain man's creative efforts. The evolutionist must regard these efforts as means to an end; but the creative artist regards his work as an end in itself. A biologist, Miss Miriam Rothschild, pointed out, for instance, that many a great genius, immensely influential in thought and in human evolution, in fact manifested a 'diseased superego':

> Rousseau was an obsessional neurotic; Van Gogh a schizophrenic; Swammerdam a melancholic; Ampère an unusual type of psychopath; John Clare a manic depressive.

Waddington's reply was that if we relate 'good' to the general course of evolution, then that solves the difficulties of the individual genius: his individual psychic balance may not have been 'good', but the course of evolution is an affair of whole species or societies:

It is just because of his contributions to the progress of mankind in general that we value such a man as Van Gogh.[1]

On which the philosopher, John Wisdom, commented decisively:

Not on your life. Social progress be damned. It's the picture that counts.[2]

Several philosophers combined forces to accuse Waddington of smuggling old-fashioned 'intuitionist' views of ethics into his account of the evolutionary process; and a psycho-analyst, Dr Karin Stephen, asked bluntly:

Is there *any* reason to suppose that evolution as a whole has the production of our 'good' mature personalities as its goal?[3]

However, in 1960 Professor Waddington, undeterred by the apparently damaging criticism of the philosophers and others, returned to the task. In his *The Ethical Animal* he restated the view of 'evolutionary ethics', this time paying attention to earlier criticisms, and above all covering a wider area of human behaviour. Thus, for instance, he took into account some of the findings of social anthropologists, like Margaret Mead. The result is a study which shows a sensitive and cultured understanding of many ranges of human activity. And I think it must be said that in most of them he does show both the possibility and the relevance of using biological analogies for developed human attitudes, re-

[1] C. H. Waddington, *Science and Ethics* (Allen & Unwin, 1942), pp. 87f.

[2] J. Wisdom in *Mind* NS LII, No. 207, July 1960.

[3] In Waddington, op. cit., p. 69.

actions and convictions. In most: but not all. He has to meet the challenge to this way of thinking which is presented by man's innate 'cussedness'. This challenge has been put, cogently, by a fellow-biologist – indeed, one of the leading world experts in genetics – T. Dobzhansky, who has urged that, however tidy a scheme of evolution we may make with man's activities falling into place within it, we must still allow for the characteristic feature of man, his waywardness, his contrariness. Tell a man he is bound to take such and such a line because evolution dictates it: the man will instantly defy evolution and do the opposite. (The point was made a hundred years ago by Dostoevsky, in his *Letters from the Underworld.*) Waddington tries to meet the challenge by arguing that there is no need to take such marginal tendencies into account when attempting to reach rational conclusions about what men *ought* to do; and further, he says that psycho-analysts have their own way of explaining why man should be 'cussed'. But this does not really solve the difficulty: it merely implies that if and when man's place in evolution is fully accepted, the cussedness will be eliminated. But some people will feel that man purged of his cussedness will not be fully man.

And it is very interesting to see how the evolutionist, even when he is trying deliberately to purge his descriptions of anthropomorphic language, finds it almost impossible to do so. We have seen that one biologist asked Waddington bluntly, 'Is there *any* reason to suppose that evolution as a whole has the production of our "good" mature personalities as its goal?' Waddington replied that there is no 'goal' of evolution (for that is an anthropomorphic, teleological concept, and 'teleology' is suspect): all we can do is to observe evolutionary change and note its characteristics. And one can see why: otherwise, an evolutionary explanation of ethics could be called circular – first ethical ideas (i.e., language of purpose, valuation, conation, etc.) are smuggled into the notion of evolution; and then evolution is used to explain the emergence of man's ethical ideas. The attempt at scientific purity is admirable. And yet the scientist can't keep it up. Thus we find Waddington writing:

> The human intellect is an instrument which has been *produced* during the course of evolution, primarily by the agency of natural selection, supplemented by the specifically human evolutionary processes. . . . Like all other products of evolution, it has been *moulded* by the necessity to fit in with . . . the rest of the natural world.

Or, on the next page, even more nakedly:

> What is demanded of an ethical theory is . . . that it should be . . . applicable to a world in which the crucial actions of a thousand million people are predicated on the belief that scientific technology is good. The intellect will have failed to carry out the functions *for which evolution designed* it if it issues merely in the conclusion that it can suggest no criteria by which one could . . . decide whether this belief has . . . validity.[1]

Dr Julian Huxley, in his famous Romanes Lecture, fell into the same trap:

> The peculiar difficulties which surround our individual

[1] C. H. Waddington, *The Ethical Animal* (Allen & Unwin, 1960), pp. 19f.

moral adjustment are seen to be largely due to our evolutionary history. Like our prolonged helplessness in infancy . . . they are a consequence of our having developed from a simian ancestry. Once we realize that the primitive super-ego is merely a makeshift developmental mechanism, no more *intended* to be the permanent central support of our morality than is our embryonic notochord *intended* to be the permanent central support of our bodily frame, we shall not take its dictates too seriously.[1]

In these three cases I have italicized the words which inescapably suggest an anthropomorphic, purposive notion. (It is, of course, notorious that the words 'natural selection' have frequently tended to carry the same charge of loaded metaphor.)

I do not cite these cases merely to score a point, but to indicate how difficult it is to escape teleological language even when trying deliberately to situate human activity within non-teleological contexts. And this difficulty surely points to the greater difficulty behind the whole undertaking. These contributions towards an 'evolutionary ethics' (particularly Waddington's) are valuable – it will not do for theologians to dismiss them.[2] But try as they will to contain the human spirit and enterprise within these evolutionary categories, something of them refuses to be so contained. And even Professor Waddington himself concedes, in his last book, that there is one aspect of the human animal that seems not to be re-

[1] J. S. Huxley, *Evolution and Ethics* (Pilot Press, 1947): cited in E. H. Erikson, 'The Roots of Virtue' in J. S. Huxley (ed.), *The Humanist Frame* (Allen & Unwin, 1961), p. 148.

[2] Cf. E. L. Mascall, *Up and Down in Adria* (Faith Press, 1963), p. 55.

ducible to any purely evolutionary explanation – the fact of self-awareness. In this phenomenon of self-awareness we confront, he says, a

> basic mystery which lies at the heart of our whole life. It is not only the experience of free-will which is inextricably involved with self-awareness; our whole understanding of the external world is deduced from what we consciously perceive.

And since the nature of self-awareness 'completely resists our understanding' he admits that the natural philosophy of biology itself faces us with the conclusion that

> however much we may understand certain aspects of the world, the very fact of existence as we know it in our experience is essentially a mystery.[1]

He hastens to add (lest he seem to his fellow-scientists to be selling out to 'mystery') that man's methods of apprehending his surroundings must have been evolved like his other functions, and that this evolution must have depended on natural selection – selection for efficiency of operation. The handle of a scythe or the shape of a knife blade have been determined by use – but this does not lead us to mistrust them: nor should we distrust the mentality of animals just because it has become shaped by use during evolution. His conclusion, however, is a modest one: that though we must recognize an essential mysteriousness in the universe, this realization does not stand alone:

> It is complemented by our confidence that the faculties

[1] Waddington, *The Nature of Life* (Allen & Unwin, 1961), p. 123.

we have for dealing with our surroundings must have at least a considerable degree of effectiveness.[1]

With this basically humble claim – so different from the *bravura* of early positivism and evolutionary scientism – we may leave the world of biological concepts of development for the world of man's moral action.

III. *Morals and Autonomy*

Ethical theory in the West during this century has tended to develop in at least two apparently divergent directions. On the one hand there has been the 'evolutionary ethics' which we have been considering (and by this I include not merely the thought of the biologists, but of anthropologists and social scientists about ethics). But on the other there has been the stress on the 'autonomy of ethics'. This latter is not a new notion; in one form or another it is as old as the Greeks. But, reinforced especially by the growth in psychological knowledge, it has acquired an importance it has hardly had before. And it can be presented in a form which constitutes not only a powerful claim for 'secular ethics' as the only appropriate formulation for 'man come of age', but also a direct challenge to Christian or any other form of theological ethics.

The challenge has been excellently expressed in a paper, 'Morality: Religious and Secular', by the con-

[1] Waddington, op. cit., p. 125. But in a discussion with Lord Halsbury in recent issues of *Philosophy* Professor Waddington defends his original position on 'Naturalism in Ethics and Biology': see *Philosophy*, Jan. 1962 (XXXVII/139), Oct. 1962 (XXXVII/142) and July 1963 (XXXVIII/145).

temporary philosopher, Professor P. H. Nowell-Smith, published recently in the *Rationalist Annual*.[1] Nowell-Smith opens unambiguously by stating his claim that religious morality is 'infantile'.

> I am well aware that this will sound absurd. To suggest that Aquinas and Kant – to say nothing of millions of Christians of lesser genius – never grew up is surely to put oneself out of court as a philosopher. . . . My thesis is not so crude as that; I shall try to show that, in the moralities of adult Christians, there are elements which can be set apart from the rest and are, indeed, inconsistent with them, that these elements can properly be called 'religious', and that just these elements are infantile.

He explains that, though indeed most people learn their moral ideas from parents, teachers, social mores, and so on, they will not have achieved an adult morality until they can accept these standards for themselves. Whereas, he claims, the distinctive characteristic of a religious ethic is that it is an ethic of command:

> Morality, on this view, is an affair of being commanded to behave in certain ways by some person who has a right to issue such commands; and, once this premise is granted, it is said with some reason that only God has such a right. Morality must be based on religion, and a morality not so based, or one based on the wrong religion, lacks all validity. It is this premise, that being moral consists in obedience to commands, that I deny.

His denial, that being moral consists in obedience to commands, is based partly on the well-known ethical position

[1] P. H. Nowell-Smith, 'Morality: Religious and Secular' in *The Rationalist Annual* 1961 (Rationalist Press Assoc.).

of the 'autonomy of ethics' – stated in other terms as the impossibility of deducing an 'ought' from an 'is', an ethical imperative from an existential statement. 'Suppose', Nowell-Smith puts it, 'that I have satisfied myself that God has commanded me to do this or that thing . . . it still makes *sense* for me to ask whether or not I *ought* to do it.' Even if we assume that God is omnipotent and omniscient, 'we must be persuaded *independently* of his goodness before we admit his right to command'. Suppose we assume that the Bible gives us the commands of this omniscient and omnipotent deity: yet

> we must judge for ourselves whether the Bible is the inspired word of a just and benevolent God or a curious amalgam of profound wisdom and gross superstition. To judge this is to make a moral decision, so that in the end, so far from morality being based on religion, religion is based on morality.

In other words, to say of a God who makes moral demands on us that he is a 'good' God we have already to have a notion of 'good' independent of those moral demands, unless we want to involve ourselves in the vicious circle of saying that what God commands is good because he commands it, and that we know this is so because the God who commands is a good God.

All this is familiar enough to moral philosophers. But Nowell-Smith's strength is that he backs up this familiar argument by an appeal to fact: the fact of infant-training. He bases himself largely upon the well-known studies of the French psychologist, Piaget. Piaget made a detailed study of children of different ages playing marbles. From this he was able to describe three stages. In the earliest stage the small child just throws the marbles around: he is playing, but not playing a 'game'. Towards the end of this stage he may start imitating older children, and therefore to some extent obeying the 'rules' of marble-playing: but he does not recognize them as 'rules', indeed, he does not know what 'rules' are. We may, says Nowell-Smith, 'call this the pre-moral attitude to rules'.

But next comes the second stage, with children from about five to nine years of age. During this stage, said Piaget,

> The rules are regarded as sacred and inviolable, emanating from adults and lasting for ever. Every suggested alteration in the rules strikes the child as a transgression.

Piaget calls this stage 'heteronomous', i.e., a stage at which rules are simply given from outside, and accepted as such. It corresponds to 'deontological ethics', i.e. that which must be done simply because it is one's duty to do it. The child knows what a 'rule' is, and indeed obeys it with punctilious and jealous exactitude, almost as if it was holy; but he does not know what a rule is 'for'.

But finally comes the last stage, from about ten years of age onward: the rule, says Piaget,

> is now looked upon as a law due to mutual consent, which you must respect if you want to be loyal, but which it is permissible to alter on condition of enlisting the general opinion of your side.

He calls this the 'autonomous' stage: though the rules have, indeed, been handed down by older children they are not irreformable. From 'this is how we learned to play' they no longer, as at the earlier stage, deduce 'this is how we ought to play'. The purpose of rules is beginning to be clear, so that this stage corresponds to 'teleological ethics': rules which exist merely to make the game playable, and which can be adapted in the light of the purpose for which they are formulated (e.g., in the case of marbles the rules may have to be altered if there is no flat surface to play on, if the numbers of players are larger, and the marbles fewer, than normally, etc.).

The comparison with religious, and specifically with Christian, ethics is obvious. It is true, says Nowell-Smith, that there are elements of 'autonomy' and of 'teleology' in Western Christian ethics: but these are not the elements which are specifically Christian. Indeed, they can be traced to the Greeks, and Nowell-Smith uses the term 'the Greek view of morality' for a teleological morality

> in which moral rules are considered to be subordinate to ends, to be rules *for* achieving ends and consequently to be judged by their tendency to promote those ends,

as contrasted with deontological morality

> in which moral rules are thought of as absolute, as categorical imperatives in no way depending for their validity on the good or bad consequences of obedience, and in which moral goodness is thought to lie in conformity to these rules for their own sake.

The Hebrew-Christian moral system particularly, based as it is on the notion of obedience to God as a Father, is a supreme example of 'heteronomous ethics' – and this means, ethics fixated at the second infantile stage. In the last resort, pure Christian ethics is only appropriate for the years between five and nine.

Similar conclusions from Piaget's observation of children's games[1] are drawn, at a more strictly psychoanalytical level, by the American psychologist, Thomas S. Szasz: and they result in a more overt challenge to those elements in Western morals which derive from the Judaeo-Christian tradition. Szasz asks bluntly, 'Where did the idea originate that the rules of the game of life ought to be so defined that those who are weak, disabled or ill should be helped?' And his reply is that 'This is the game usually played in childhood'. But this 'game' itself derives from 'the dominant religions of Western man. Judaism, and especially Christianity, teach these rules.' In the Bible,

> the motif that God loves the humble, the needy, or those who fear Him is a thread running through both the Old and the New Testaments.... This attitude, which amounts to nothing less than a dread of happiness or contentment, is fundamental to the psychology of the person who participates in the Judaeo-Christian ethic. The defensive, self-protective character of this 'masochistic' manoeuvre is evident.... The *Sermon on the Mount* (Matt. 5.1-12) is probably the best illustration of the rules fostering dependency and disability.[2]

And Szasz refers, as illustrations of this prolongation of childhood, to the various 'religious inhibitions on knowledge': for eating the fruit of the tree of knowledge, he says, man was expelled from the Garden; and such institutions as the Roman Catholic 'Index of Prohibited

[1] Piaget, *The Moral Judgement of the Child* (1932) and *Judgement and Reasoning in the Child* (1952), passim.

[2] T. S. Szasz, *The Myth of Mental Illness* (Secker, 1961), pp. 193, 196.

Books', or such phenomena as 'national narcissisms', racial prejudice, etc., are all a 'fostering of infantilism'.[1] Szasz's main purpose in his book is not, as it might seem from these brief quotations, to criticize religious traditions, but to question current assumptions about 'mental health' and 'mental illness'. 'Much of what passes for "medical ethics"', he says challengingly, 'is a set of rules the net effect of which is the persistent infantilization and subjugation of the patient.' The connection between this his main theme (that 'mental illness' is a myth) and the Western religious tradition, is that 'men learn how to be "mentally ill" by following (mainly) the rules of these two games' – *sc.*, of the family and of religion: and he quotes Freud in support, who frequently stressed that man's prolonged childhood is responsible for his proneness to 'neurosis', because man wants to remain a child.[2] This leads Szasz to a 'tough-minded' ethics which dissociates itself quite deliberately from the 'soft-minded' infantilism of Christian ethics. We may compare what another psychologist (Miss M. Brierley), quoted earlier, said:

> It is to Christianity that the civilized West, though not the East, owes its conviction that aggression is evil in itself. Non-recognition of aggression as a natural, pre-moral force, having its appropriate uses as well as its too frequent abuses, is, in part, responsible for the Christian failure to solve the problems of aggression. . . . By reason of its very nature, an idealistic ethic should not be expected to provide a stable solution of any profoundly real human problem.[3]

[1] Szasz, op. cit., p. 186. [2] Ibid., pp. 183, 185.
[3] M. Brierley, *Trends in Psychoanalysis*, p. 282.

The Moral Animal

Let us frankly admit that 'Christian' ethics have too often given the impression of over-submissiveness. Or, to put it another way: how would traditional Christian ethics fit the following moving episode into its schema? It is a true incident, quoted in Bruno Bettelheim's fascinating book on the psychology of Auschwitz 'Extermination Camp', *The Informed Heart*:

> Once, a group of naked prisoners about to enter the gas chamber stood lined up in front of it. In some way the commanding SS officer learned that one of the women prisoners had been a dancer. So he ordered her to dance for him. She did, and as she danced, she approached him, seized his gun, and shot him down. She, too, was immediately shot to death. (Quoted from Kogon, *Der SS-Staat*, p. 132.)[1]

And Bettelheim's comment on this heroic action is

> Isn't it possible that despite the grotesque setting in which she danced, dancing made her once again a person? Dancing, she was singled out as an individual, asked to perform in what had once been her chosen vocation. No longer was she a number, a nameless, depersonalized prisoner, but the dancer she used to be. Transformed, however momentarily, she responded like her old self, destroying the enemy bent on her destruction, even if she had to die in the process. . . . Exercising the last freedom that not even the concentration camp could take away – to decide how one wishes to think and feel about the conditions of one's life – this dancer threw off her real prison. This she could do because she was willing to risk her life to achieve autonomy once more. If we do that, then if we cannot live, at least we die like men.

Is it the unregenerate self in us which rises – despite

[1] B. Bettelheim, *The Informed Heart* (Thames & Hudson, 1961), pp. 264f.

any biblical rules of 'thou shalt not kill' – to acclaim such an action? Or can this sort of 'sanctified aggression' (for which, after all, there are plenty of precedents in the Old Testament, from Jail the wife of Heber the Kenite, on) be found a place in our Christian books of moral theology?

We are back, at any rate, at Professor Nowell-Smith's emphasis upon autonomy. It is clear what such an emphasis is a reaction against. If I take an example from Roman Catholic moral theology it is only because the particular example is the clearest illustration I can find. It would not be difficult to discover examples from other Christian traditions too. In February 1963 a correspondent to the *Clergy Review* propounded a question about the use of contraceptives, forbidden of course to Roman Catholics. The question concerns the (Roman Catholic) wife of a husband who insists on using a condom in sexual intercourse: must she refuse intercourse, and if so, what is to be the extent of her refusal? The questioner quoted a Fr F. J. Connell, who had earlier said on this problem:

> It is the duty of the wife to refuse her husband even to the extent of employing physical resistance. Only when it is truly probable that some grave injury will be inflicted on her by her husband if she resists . . . may the wife passively allow him to perform the act, just as a girl who is being raped may abstain from physical resistance if she fears that it will only stimulate the attacker to injure or to kill her. She may not consent to the pleasure of the act.

And the questioner asks, on this basis, whether this

same argument would not justify the wife in submitting because of fear lest the continuous strain of having either to resist or separate will induce a nervous breakdown?

To this the official moral theologian of the *Clergy Review*, Fr L. L. McReavey, replies in the negative. He quotes not only the decree of the Sacred Penitentiary, but some twenty modern authors who have written on the subject. He refers to a number of opinions which imply that 'passive unresisting admission entails formal complicity'. The wife, as in the case of rape, must offer positive physical resistance '*totis viribus*'. But he admits that the authorities differ on the point at which she may lawfully discontinue physical resistance. Some hold that she must first be 'physically overpowered', or that her resistance must extend to the utmost of her power, i.e., until the other's greater strength wins. However, they agree that *fear* of a grave enough evil to herself may be adequate to justify her non-resistance. In the case of the wife, the fear or threat of adultery by the husband, if she does not give way, is *not* a sufficient reason for her allowing him to use a contraceptive: otherwise this threat could be used by the husband to obtain anything he wanted. For he will argue, 'Does my pious wife oppose me? Then I will tell her I intend to commit adultery if she won't give way, and then she will give me what I want.' But this would lead to a co-operation by her which could hardly be distinguished from 'formal co-operation'. Fr McReavey's conclusion is that:

> A wife must resist condomistic intercourse to the limit of her physical ability, unless or until she cannot oppose or any

longer maintain effective resistance without very grave physical consequences to herself here and now.

It is difficult, therefore, he says, to see how the same could be said of a wife who submits to her husband's immoral demand through fear of some *future* consequence of present resistance, such as a nervous breakdown. On the other hand, provided she is not in proximate danger of 'consenting to the abuse', she is not obliged 'to cease cohabitation with her husband in order to deprive him of the opportunity of imposing his will on her by force'.[1]

This reply by Mgr McReavey drew forth an answer from another priest, with which I think that those who are not Roman Catholics will have considerable sympathy. He says (I summarize):

It is unfortunately true that many lay people have little confidence in the advice of priests about their marital problems, on the grounds that we (priests) have no first-hand experience of marriage. It is idle to deny that normally they are right, and one cannot help feeling that this treatment of the problem of condomistic intercourse supports their opinion. . . . I would think that this passage would make them (lay people) feel more than ever that the clergy do not understand.

The priest in such cases is dealing with people who love each other, with all the emotional and sensual attraction to each other which is included in being in love. . . . In these circumstances to equate a woman whose husband insists on the use of a condom or other appliance with a girl who is being raped is just not realistic. It has nothing to do with real life. In the former case the woman is approached by a

[1] *The Clergy Review* (Westminster), Feb. 1963 (XVIII/2), pp. 114ff.

man to whom she is strongly attracted in every way, physically and spiritually, in the latter by one for whom she feels nothing but revulsion. Where is the equality? . . .

Priests are dealing with human persons and not machines, and one cannot but feel that anyone . . . who seriously equates a loving wife with a virgin in danger of rape is out of touch with real people and real human problems.[1]

It is heartening, at least, that it should be a fellow Roman Catholic and a priest who made this protest; no doubt the secular humanist, while welcoming it, will say that it merely shows the healthy influence of secularism penetrating even to the Catholic clergy. But the reaction against a paternalistic (and 'priest-ridden') ethic in favour of an ethic of autonomy is more than a rejection of specific moral injunctions issuing from the former: it is a rejection of injunction-issuing at all. So that when the sociologist, Dr Ronald Fletcher, was asked to write about ethics for young people from a humanist point of view, the head-piece of his article states that

Rationalists in the modern world reject the authoritarian heritage of Moses and substitute a set of non-commandments, i.e. principles on which the individual must work out his own conduct when faced by particular problems.

And Dr Fletcher modestly offers a Humanist's Decalogue, of which the first Non-Commandment is

Never accept authority: whether that of a jealous god, priest, prime minister, president, dictator . . . etc., unless, in your own seriously considered view, there are good grounds for it. You are quite right to reject orthodox religions; at

[1] Fr Wilfred Stibbs in *Clergy Review*, May 1963, pp. 321f.

present (as our clergymen insist) orthodox religions are a shambles. Given the present state of knowledge, the only position of integrity you can hold is one of careful, honest, open-minded agnosticism. . . .[1]

IV. *Autonomy for Relationship*

It is clear, indeed, that whereas a hundred years ago secular humanists tended to praise Christian ethics (with mild reservations) but rejected Christian dogma, today they tend to reject the ethic and merely ignore the dogma. But we must not draw the wrong conclusions from this. I believe that it should be taken as a sign of a greater honesty (the lip-service to Christian morality paid by some Victorian and post-Victorian sceptics was sometimes dubious); and more, that it is the sign of an attempt to reach a more integral view of man.

We said above (at the beginning of section III) that a paradoxical development in the West has been in two apparently opposite directions: one towards an 'evolutionary ethic' (i.e. an ethic that sees man as part of a biological process of 'transformism'), the other towards 'autonomous ethics', of which we have quoted Nowell-Smith's account. But in fact these need not be contradictory, if we see autonomous ethics as the ethics of 'developing persons in relation'. For (*a*) man is part of a developing (evolving) society, and is of course influenced by it (Marx knew all about this); but (*b*) society is composed of men, individual men with their desires, personal decisions to make, fears and loves, etc., in fact

[1] Ronald Fletcher in *New Society* No. 31, 2nd May, 1963, pp. 17f.

autonomous men: therefore society can not be considered in abstraction from man as person.

But it is this precisely which, I think, points to the weakness of Nowell-Smith's account of, and plea for, 'autonomy'. It is curious that when he wants to find an expression to distinguish 'autonomy' from 'heteronomy', he sums up the former in the slogan 'the Sabbath was made for man, not man for the Sabbath'. And he calls this the 'Greek view of morality' – which is odd, when one remembers who was the Author of the slogan! He admits, it is true, that the New Testament, and Christianity generally, contain elements of autonomous or teleological morality: but he contends that it is the Hebrew, deontological or heteronomous elements which distinguish Christian morals from those elements in morality which are common to Christians and secular humanists. This ignores the patent fact that Christianity claims to be a religion of freedom; that the Christian doctrine of man asserts the primacy of the individual conscience; that no one can be saved against his will and that faith not freely accepted is not true faith. To this extent Christianity insists on a basic autonomy at the centre of its moral scheme.

There are three main objections to Nowell-Smith's exposition. *First*, he makes an illegitimate comparison between the growth of an individual man and the growth of peoples through history (between what the biologists call ontogeny and phylogeny). It will be remembered that he uses Piaget's three stages of game-learning among children as an analogy for the passage of man from primitive anarchy through authoritarianism (heteronomy) to self-realization (autonomy). This is, of course, only another form of Comte's three stages of history (religious, metaphysical and positive) which we discussed in chapter two. But the analogy is so inexact as to be misleading. It suggests that, if Christianity is suitable to the mental ages of five to nine, mankind is now 'come of age', is able to make its own rules. How can such a suggestion be demonstrated? How does it allow for possible regression? And even if progress is assured, does the analogy imply that societies are bound, like individuals, to pass beyond maturity to senescence? *Second*, can we be so sure of Piaget's analysis? I have quoted the American psychologist, Thomas S. Szasz in support of Nowell-Smith's identification of Hebrew-Christian ethics as 'infantile'. But Szasz also says of Piaget:

> I believe he did not stress sufficiently the ethical choices implicit in them [*sc.* the rules of the game]. . . . What Piaget described reflects . . . mainly the kind of development which some members of the middle and upper classes of contemporary Western nations would want for their own children, or for themselves.[1]

Can we be sure, that is, that from a particular piece of observation we can draw such general conclusions as Nowell-Smith does? And *third*, there seems to be some confusion about the notion of 'autonomy'. Nowell-Smith appears to identify 'autonomous' with 'teleological' ethics. (Both 'Greek'.) But teleological means, 'defined by purpose': if, then, it is purpose that explains obligation,

[1] Szasz, op. cit., p. 229.

this is surely a form of heteronomy. The purest form of autonomous ethics is that of Sartre's existentialism: man not only chooses his ends, but constructs himself. But existentialism is non-teleological: that is its whole point. (In Sartre's terminology, only the *en-soi* can be *pour autre*: the *pour-soi* can only be *pour-soi*, not *pour* anything else whatsoever, for it merely 'exists', it has no 'essence' that can be directed towards or by something else.) And Nowell-Smith is not an existentialist. Indeed, when he applies his principles of autonomy to the case of marriage, he tries to show that adultery is 'wrong' because it is an act of 'disloyalty'. The notion of 'loyalty' and 'disloyalty' is meaningless to a Sartrean existentialist. By disloyalty in marriage Nowell-Smith says he means 'an act likely to break the union which he [the husband] values'. But loyalty is surely something less self-centred than this: it must extend (if 'the life-long union of a man and a woman in the intimacy of marriage is a supreme form of love', as Nowell-Smith believes) to include loyalty to another person. And this surely means the autonomous choice of a heteronomy (the willing, mutual, submission of lovers to each other). In this sense Christians would claim that their ethic is teleological (for behind it lies God's purpose for man); it is also autonomous (for man is given his freedom by a loving, not a tyrannical, God); and it is also deontological (for man's duty is service, a service, however, 'which is perfect freedom').

I fancy that some contemporary secular thinkers in other fields would in fact endorse these three points. I refer to what I believe is an important advance in the West which, though it has been happening for some years now, has not yet had much recognition: the coming together of philosophers, political theorists and sociologists. I have referred in the last chapter to the small book on the *Idea of a Social Science* by the philosopher Peter Winch; and also to *Political Man* by S. M. Lipset. Perhaps the most useful studies for the general reader showing this trend, are *Philosophy*, *Politics and Society*, *Second Series* (ed. P. Laslett and W. G. Runciman)[1] and Runciman's own *Social Science and Political Theory*.[2] The significance of these books, and of the convergent interest which they betoken, is that they show the possibility of establishing real and fruitful connections between different disciplines which had been isolated from each other, to their own loss. And the result of this collaboration is a much more sensitive understanding of the complexities of a man's motivation in his socio-political behaviour. Thus Mr Runciman is concerned to show the importance of several recent studies of 'voting behaviour' for political theorists. These studies all suggest that a-priori dogmatism about political systems must give way before the facts about human participation in politics. If, for instance, the sociologist is right who concluded that 'voters do not decide issues'; or if, according to another, 'stable poverty is the best guarantee of conservatism'; or if, according to a third, 'habit'

[1] P. Laslett and W. G. Runciman (eds.), *Philosophy*, *Politics and Society*, *Second Series* (Blackwell, 1962).

[2] W. G. Runciman, *Social Science and Political Theory* (C.U.P., 1963).

largely dictates voting, and few voters change their political allegiances: if these are true, then the political theorist must take note of 'how unlike the process of voting is to a rational choice between considered alternatives'.[1] It would seem that some social and political theorists, through neglecting the power of symbolic thinking – the influence of imagination over fact – in human choices and motives, have done less than justice to the way in which men behave in society or politics. Since untrue theories about men in society can lead to mistaken prescriptions for them, this joint thinking between philosophers, sociologists and political theorists is likely to lead to a more balanced and reliable humanism. And it will tend to correct the over-intellectualist view of 'autonomy' presented by philosophers like Nowell-Smith.

For man is more than a spectator, merely making selections from what he sees, on the basis of which he can act. He is also subject, and that means accepting (freely accepting) authority. He is comrade, needing and finding fulfilment in fellowship. He is also participant, needing commitment. And this carries a corollary, which again is not fully catered for in the intellectualistic ethics of autonomy: there is room in this latter for error, but hardly for rebellion. Yet man, to be fully man, must be free not only to choose the right, to select his purposes, but also to choose the wrong, and even (so far as that is indeed possible to him) to refuse to choose at all.

[1] Runciman, op. cit., p. 42.

5

Man the Rebel

›››◆‹‹‹

I. *Science and Psychology*

THERE is another kind of humanism which does allow for the rebellious element in man. It is not the dominant form, and indeed it is a little surprising that the dominant form of secular humanism (as represented, for instance, by Professor Nowell-Smith's position, discussed in the last chapter) appears to pay so little attention to this profounder, less anaemic, more inclusive form. One of the leading American literary critics, Lionel Trilling, said of Freud:

> One is always aware in reading Freud how little cynicism there is in his thought. His desire for man is only that he should be human, and to this end his science is devoted. The view of life to which the artist responds can insure the quality of his work, but the poetic qualities of Freud's own principles, which are so clearly in the line of the classic tragic realism, suggest that this is a view which does not narrow and simplify the human world for the artist but on the contrary opens and complicates it.[1]

One is aware of a faint sense of embarrassment in secular humanist circles when Freud is mentioned: 'He obviously should be one of us' – this is the impression given – 'and yet he does say such awful things: not

[1] Lionel Trilling, *The Liberal Imagination* (Secker, 1951), pp. 5-7.

quite nice really (all this about universal human neurosis); fortunately we have the neo-Freudians nearby and they can bowdlerize him for us. And anyway, old Sigmund – a bit *vieux jeu*, isn't he, a bit pre-scientific? . . . '

It is true that the strictly scientific character of psycho-analysis is being sternly challenged in our day. Estimates seem to suggest that possibly some sixty per cent of patients treated by psycho-analytic methods have 'improved': but other studies (e.g. in America) show nearly seventy per cent discharged as 'recovered or improved' after little or no psychiatric treatment. This is in line with the figures given for ECT (electro-convulsive therapy): patients treated with mild shocks, inducing unconsciousness but not convulsions, though under the belief that they were getting shocks, improved just as well as those who were shocked.[1] The best one can say, therefore, about psycho-analysis as a therapy is that its effectiveness by comparison with other methods of treatment is 'unproven'. It is certainly significant that in Great Britain (according to one estimate) of some 350 analysts over 270 are Freudians, but against this there are 2,400 psychiatrists, who are presumably eclectic in their methods.

I do not think, however, that Freud would have been depressed by these figures. In the first place, the influence of his classic researches has been far wider than any counting of heads according to 'schools' could

[1] Figures given by B. A. Farrell, 'Psycho-analysis: The Method' in *New Society* No. 39, 27th June, 1963; and citing studies by H. J. Eysenck, C. Landix, N. Q. Brill and others.

indicate. (I suspect that even Dr Eysenck, the most vigorous opponent of 'Freudianism' in favour of a more 'scientific' approach, has not been able wholly to purge all Freudian categories from psychological theory.) And secondly, as Dr Bowlby has pointed out, Freud regarded his theories as provisional, subject to testing, and discardable as soon as they could be proved by empirical observation to be untrue. He quotes Freud himself as saying:

> A science erected on empirical interpretation . . . will gladly content itself with nebulous, scarcely imaginable basic concepts which it hopes [either] to apprehend more clearly in the course of its development, or . . . to replace by others. For these ideas are not the foundation of science (which) is observation alone . . . but the top of the whole structure and they can be replaced and discarded without damaging it.[1]

And again, Freud emphasized that his 'metapsychology' (i.e., his psycho-analytical theory) was

> part of a speculative superstructure of psycho-analysis, any portion of which can be abandoned or changed without loss or regret the moment its inadequacy has been proved.[2]

And finally, the profoundest contribution of Freud to our culture has been in his understanding, not merely of the mentally ill but of every man in his or her unconscious self: and this can be valid whatever the success or unsuccess of therapeutic methods elaborated on the basis of this understanding. The fact that *Placebos* can in many illnesses effect as swift a cure as genuine drugs

[1] J. Bowlby (of Tavistock Clinic) in *New Society* No. 41, 11th July, 1963, quoting Freud, *On Narcissism* (1914).

[2] Bowlby, art. cit., quoting Freud, *Autobiographical Study* (1925).

may throw doubt upon some pharmacological predictions but cannot disrupt the whole basis of pathology. The epoch-making investigations of Freud are almost, one could say, more valuable for the 'normal' man than for the neurotic.

II. *The Psycho-analytic Challenge*

One of the most penetrating French literary critics of this century, for many years editor of the *Nouvelle Revue Française*, used to link together two names which might seem to be very disparate: Freud and Proust. This critic, Jacques Rivière, was one of the first Frenchmen to see that Proust was a genius – at a time when the majority of even his most distinguished confrères were dismissing this new-fangled, valetudinarian novelist as a charlatan. But Rivière also saw the importance of Freud's investigations: and though he conceded that Proust might never have read Freud, he spent much time in showing that their contributions were parallel, even complementary. He puts his finger on the dominant idea behind Proust's long novel:

> The idea which is latent everywhere in his work, the idea akin to that of Freud, that the primary function of our feelings is to lie to us and that the first duty of the psychologist, of the writer, is to resist the evidence they give concerning themselves, and the guise in which they seek to appear before our eyes.

And, with what may seem to some a terrible, almost a gloating, cynicism, Rivière explains what he takes to be Proust's greatest illumination for us:

In contact with Proust, we realized to what extent man is an artist in deceiving himself about himself, and little by little each of us watched our instinctive and quite imaginary picture of our own soul come unstuck from the real soul. Under his influence, the natural, congenital hypocrisy of feelings revealed itself gradually of its own accord. We saw what our friendship for him made us capable of, but we also saw that point beyond which it did not give us the strength to go on. . . . As far as I am concerned, Proust has probably been the most terrifying revealer of myself that I could ever encounter. One feels the depths that he opens up. And how quietly! Without ill will or bitterness . . . fully aware of what the dream can include, extending rather than diminishing the resources of the soul, he simply shows in addition that illusion which sustains our life. . . Proust and Freud initiate a new way of questioning consciousness.[1]

This is a remarkable passage to have been written in the early twenties; but all that Rivière says about Proust could be said about Freud too.

Freud is, as we have seen, criticized by the statistical school of psychology today, which regards his 'hunches' as unscientific because they do not emerge from a careful factorization of empirical data. But what is more curious is that he is also criticized by the physiological or chemical school of psychology for the same lack of an empirical basis – this time a physio-chemical one. More curious, because Freud himself started off from precisely their position, and only veered away from it when he found it left many psychological phenomena (slips of the tongue, dreams, etc.) unexplained. Indeed, he was accused in his

[1] Jacques Rivière, *The Ideal Reader* (Harvill, 1961), pp. 127, 129-30.

own day (by Jung and others), as he still is by the neo-Freudians, of being too biologically biased in his approach.

It is easy to see the force of these objections to Freud and even to sympathize with them. As one thinks of the expense (of time as well as money) of a full course of psycho-analysis; as (worse) one thinks of the sort of people who *can* afford such a course, and speculates how little good to the world even a complete 'cure' of such a patient would be likely to effect; and then as one looks at the statistics of the mentally unwell, calculating the available resources in hospitals and psychiatric staff – then one is tempted to think of the psycho-analytic movement as a great, otiose, irrelevant side-show. Faced with the vast problems of mental health, isn't it natural to feel some impatience with the elaborate and costly apparatus devoted to helping (and not always that) the few; and to long instead for a good, solid, laboratory-tested therapy for the many, based on properly verified hypotheses?

But this kind of impatience is to be resisted: not only because it is based on mere expediency – and a policy based on expediency alone is always shaky; but also because, as we have said, if psycho-analysis is true, it is true about man, not merely about sick man – and truth does not require any justification outside itself.

And much of what Freud's case-histories reveal seems to me true, in this self-justifying way, in two senses. First, the analyses are so often cogent in a way that makes the demand for statistical proof irrelevant. When you uncover for me the pattern of life of a specific individual, in such a way that I at once recognize that individual from what I already know of him, I am satisfied – I don't want any further statistics about him. And second, Freud seems to me to illuminate elements in the human person which neither the behaviouristic nor the physio-chemical accounts of man get at: by comparison, these last seem like using a quarter-inch probe to investigate an organ of one-inch diameter.

What is it specially that Freud uncovers? Jacques Rivière has stated it well: the power of illusion and the ubiquity of self-deception. As one of Freud's most intelligent contemporary defenders, Mr Philip Rieff, has said:

> His instinctualism is chiefly what gives an admirable sharpness to his estimate of human nature, and makes it more valuable as a defense of the individual than the critique of his position theoretically prefigured by (John) Dewey and carried out by such neo-Freudians as Karen Horney and Erich Fromm or than the present-centred psychology of Adler, which blames society for the characteristic frustrations of the individual. The liberal revisers of Freud, in their efforts to avoid the pessimistic implications of his genetic reasoning, tend to let the ideas of the individual be absorbed into the social, or at best to permit it a vague and harried existence. Freud himself – through his mythology of the instincts – kept some part of character safe from society, restoring to the idea of human nature a hard core, not easily warped or reshaped by social experience.[1]

It may seem something of a paradox to say that Freud's emphasis upon the instincts as the basis of psychic life protects the individual. But I think Mr Rieff is right:

[1] Philip Rieff, *Freud: The Mind of the Moralist* (Gollancz, 1960), p. 33.

if you trace all failures of personality, as a social philosopher like John Dewey does, to some failure in the individual's relation to society, some hiatus in his social habit, then you will tend to think of social engineering as the main way to improvement of the individual. Freud was not so optimistic, and here lies the value of his realism. Rieff says again:

> Given his dialectic of progress and regress in character, Freud has been viewed as being on the whole pessimistic about the chances of individual improvement. The neo-Freudians accuse him of denying, through his mainly biological orientation, the importance of the individual's positive powers of growth and maturity. But his 'instinctualism' or 'biologism' is his way of expressing the more fundamental idea, sacrificed by his revisers, of human behaviour, conceived as *conflict*, by uncompromisingly posing instinct against those forces, within the self as well as in society, which block its development, Freud preserves the most vital function of the individual.

And I am bound to register my agreement with Rieff here when he concludes that

> His [Freud's] dark vision of the embattled self seems to me truer than the cheery platitudes of his revisers, who assure us that what we need to solve our problems is 'genuine warmth and affection' from parents, or better living through a cessation of 'excessive demands on the environment' (Horney), or learning to cooperate with 'rational authority' while rejecting 'irrational authority' (Fromm). The goals set by the neo-Freudians – the goal of 'actualizing' or 'realizing' our full potentialities for 'productiveness', 'maturity', 'freedom', 'spontaneity' – conceal a wholesale sacrifice of what is challenging and serious in the Freudian insights.[1]

[1] Rieff, op. cit., p. 56.

The result is that 'on the whole Freud stands with Hobbes, as opposed to Rousseau; not that man is good and society corrupts him, but that man is anarchic and society restrains him'.[1] But he has nothing of Hobbes' cynicism: for Freud allows for love and freedom, as well as mere force and cunning, and above all allows for 'the law of "primal ambivalence", which provides every strong hate with a counterpart of love, and hobbles every act of aggression with a subsequent burden of guilt'.

It is true that Freud's early neurological training, and his inheritance of nineteenth-century mechanistic scientism, result constantly in language which sounds uncompromisingly deterministic. I'm afraid we cannot exonerate him from this, when we can find him speaking of 'the thorough-going meaningfulness and determinism of even the apparently most obscure and arbitrary mental phenomena', etc. But central to his purpose was the aim which he summed up as 'where *id* was, there *ego* shall be',[2] and this implies a notion of freedom which seems to contradict his determinism. As Mr Alasdair MacIntyre says, in a useful little philosophical study of the Unconscious:

> 'Cure' for Freud means more than the mitigation of neurotic symptoms, which is what it tends to mean for those who apply physical methods in psychiatry. To be cured is to have become reasonable, aware of the true nature of one's situation, able to cope with it instead of being overcome by it. . . .

[1] Rieff, op. cit., p. 221, note.

[2] Freud, *New Introductory Lectures* (Inst. of Psycho-analysis, 1933), p. 106.

And again,

> Freud is so often presented as undermining the rationalist conception of man as a self-sufficient, self-aware, self-controlled being, that we are apt to forget that although he may have abandoned such a conception as an account of what man is, he never retreated from it as an account of what man ought to be. . . . Freud's whole recognition of unconscious purposes is a discovery that men are more, not less, rational than we thought they were. His whole method of treatment rests on the assertion that men can face and cope with their situation rationally, if only they are given the opportunity. Freud himself helps to conceal this from us by his vehement disavowal of any moralistic purpose in his work. Nonetheless he promotes a moral ideal for which rationality is central.[1]

For indeed, his therapy always assumes that reasonableness is better than prejudice, mastering hate better than giving way to it, sympathy and objectivity better than blindness about our own behaviour and that of others, etc. And at one point Freud himself in effect admits the limitations of his deterministic interpretations. Discussing a case of female homosexuality, he observes:

> So long as we trace the development from its final outcome backwards, the chain of events appears continuous, and we feel we have gained an insight which is completely satisfactory or even exhaustive. But if we proceed the reverse way, if we start from premises inferred from the analysis and try to follow these up to the final result, then we no longer get the impression of an inevitable sequence of events which could not have been otherwise determined. We notice

[1] A. MacIntyre, *The Unconscious* (Routledge, 1958), pp. 91-3.

at once that we might have been just as well able to understand and explain the latter.[1]

Of course Freud had his personal weaknesses – Jung has revealed some of these in his posthumously published autobiography. Whether his famous 'anti-feminism' is as exaggerated as the present generation likes to make out, is a disputed point. There is less doubt that along with his profound respect for the sexual act Freud had a curious, almost puritanical distaste for its manifestations – as Rieff says, 'There is no trace of the lyrical in his analysis of the sexual instinct and its satisfactions'. And for an example he quotes Freud saying (had D. H. Lawrence ever read this?):

> Excremental things are all too intimately and inseparably bound up with sexual things; the position of the genital organs – 'inter urinas et faeces' – remains the decisive and unchangeable factor. . . . As the genitals themselves have not undergone the development of the rest of the human form in the direction of beauty, [but] have retained their animal cast . . . [so] even today love, too, is in essence as animal as ever it was.[2]

His rationalism resulted in the fact that, though he enjoyed novels, plays, painting and sculpture (poetry less), he took no interest in music. A. A. Brill says that he 'rebelled against being moved by something without knowing why; and as he could not discover the meaning of music, he was almost incapable of obtaining any

[1] Freud, 'The Psychogenesis of a Case of Homosexuality in a Woman', 1920 (Standard Edit. XVIII/167): cited in Rieff, op. cit., pp. 116-7.

[2] Freud, 'On the Universal Tendency to Debasement in the Sphere of Love', 1912 (Standard Edit. XI/183, 215): cited in Reiff, p. 121.

pleasure from it'.[1] He accepted, too, rather uncritically, the findings of such anthropologists as Frazer and Tylor, and built elaborate theories of psychogenesis upon their rather flimsy foundations. (Though it is interesting to find him differing from the majority view in favour of a primitive monotheism which in fact has found a few supporters among professional anthropologists since.) And perhaps the most glaring weakness is in his treatment of religion – on which Rieff says 'against no other strongpoint of representative culture are the reductive weapons of psycho-analysis deployed in such open hostility. Freud's customary detachment fails him here.'[2] It is indeed possible that there was some slight neurotic element in his strong anti-religious reactions. We can not forget the story he told himself about his youth: how his father recounted that a Christian had once knocked off his cap and ordered, 'Jew! get off the pavement'.

> 'And what did you do?' I asked.
>
> 'I went into the roadway and picked up my cap,' was his quiet reply. This struck me as unheroic conduct on the part of the big, strong man who was holding the little boy by the hand. I contrasted this situation with another which fitted my feelings better: the scene in which Hannibal's father, Hamilcar Barca, made his boy swear before the household altar to take vengeance on the Romans. Ever since that time Hannibal has had a place in my fantasies.[3]

And Rieff points out that in fact Freud argues in a circle about religion: having defined religious feelings as those

[1] A. A. Brill, *Freud's Contribution to Psychiatry* (Norton, N.Y., 1944): Rieff, p. 121. [2] Rieff, p. 257.

[3] Freud, *The Interpretation of Dreams* (Standard Edit. IV/197): Rieff, p. 261.

of dependence and submission, he then dismisses religion by referring its feelings to their origin in the child-parent situation; and if you claim that there are other elements in the religious complex he disallows these as 'intellectual dilutions or displacements of the primary infantile sentiments'. Which reminds one of the Soviet guide declaring to visitors that the churches in Russia are frequented only by 'old people'; and when a visitor objects, 'But I saw several young people in a church in Tomsk' (or wherever), the guide replies 'They were old people'.

But from Freud's own teaching about the ambivalence of mythology and the nature of repression we should not be surprised at the nature of his own anti-religious bias. For in spite of his constant efforts, and claims, to speak in a strictly scientific language, much of Freud's explanation is in fact mythological. And herein lies much of his greatness: for the mythopoeic faculty (as Coleridge called it) is precisely one of the creative elements in man's make-up. Someone has said that with his *Id*, *Ego* and *Super-Ego*, Freud has 'provided a demonology for modern man'. And I believe that his use of dramatic, semi-personified language helps him to convey to us the realities of the human struggle in a way which more exact (or would-be exact), impersonal language could not do. And it is this, too, which mitigates Freud's pessimism and his apparent fatalism. He may, indeed, show the inherent weakness of the self, and the threefold burden it bears of discordant impulses, unappeased conflicts and unsolved doubts. But, says Rieff:

> Freud was not fatalistic. He used a military metaphor. The ego is an army besieged on three fronts. 'We must come to its aid.' The 'civil war' which is neurosis may be resolved. The siege of the ego may be lifted by the analyst, who is the ego's 'ally from without'.[1]

But, Rieff insists, this does not imply

> a genuinely tragic view of personality. The submission to fate of which tragedy consisted in preceding ages, means something very different in the age of science. A tragic view does not put an emphasis such as Freud put on the control and manipulation of everyday life, the care and deployment of one's psychological forces. The undertone of tragedy in his doctrine of immutable conflict has superimposed upon it the comic solvent, therapy.[2]

This leads to the element which Freud developed late on in his work – the element which has probably had more scorn poured upon it than any other in his system: the so-called 'Death-Wish'. Freud complained that a failure by society to face reality, including and above all the reality of death, resulted only in frivolity. Civilized morality had tended to 'put death on one side'. When, said Freud, the 'highest stake in the game of living, life itself, may not be risked', then life becomes impoverished and uninteresting: it becomes, in Freud's graphic language,

> as shallow and empty as . . . an American flirtation, in which it is understood from the first that nothing is to happen, as

[1] Freud, *An Outline of Psychoanalysis*: Rieff, pp. 46-7, 36.

[2] Rieff, p. 63. Contrast Trilling, p. 120; but he implies different definition of tragedy.

contrasted with a Continental love-affair in which both partners must constantly bear its serious consequences in mind.[1]

A more studied awareness of death would teach us more about the seriousness of living: 'Death will no longer be denied; we are forced to believe in it.'[2]

III. *Death*

So far I have leaned heavily upon Philip Rieff's excellent study. But at this point the argument is driven home even more forcibly in another exposition of Freud which for all its occasional over-emphasis or even extravagance, is valuable and ought not to be neglected, above all by Christians: Norman O. Brown's *Life Against Death*.[3] At the end of our last chapter we suggested that the intellectualistic account of man, the 'moral animal', is inadequate. And this led us to the present discussion of psychology, as giving a fuller picture of the human state. Dr Brown interestingly points out that there is a contradiction, or at least a contrast, between two views of man's end, which goes back to Plato himself: in most of his work Plato thinks of the *summum bonum* for man as 'contemplation' (*theoria*), contemplation of the forms or ideas.

But ambiguously juxtaposed with this doctrine of man as contemplator is the Platonic doctrine of Eros, which, as elaborated by Plato in the *Symposium* and the *Phaedrus*,

[1] Freud, *Thoughts for the Times on War and Death* (Standard Edit. XIV/289f.).

[2] Freud, ibid., p. 291: cited in Rieff, p. 312.

[3] Norman O. Brown, *Life against Death* (Routledge, 1959).

suggests that the fundamental quest of man is to find a satisfactory object for his love.[1]

It is this latter element in Plato which (as it were) foreshadows Freud. For 'it is a Freudian axiom that the essence of man consists, not, as Descartes maintained, in thinking, but in desiring'.

This leads to a critique of Christianity:

> Christian theology (or at least Augustinian theology), recognised restlessness and discontent . . . as the psychological source of the historical process. But Christian theology . . . has to take man out of the real world . . . and inculcate into him delusions of grandeur. And thus Christian theology commits its own worst sin, the sin of pride. Freud's real critique of religion in *The Future of an Illusion* is the contention . . . that true humility lies in science. [We have to] learn from Copernicus that the human world is not the purpose or the center of the universe; . . . from Darwin that man is a member of the animal kingdom; and . . . from Freud that the human ego is not even master in its own house.[2]

But it is not only religion that is criticized: the easier, more optimistic versions of psychology come even more severely under fire. In fact, Dr Brown's view is that:

> It takes only the capacity to endure unpleasant truth to prefer the bleak pessimism of *Civilization and its Discontents* to the lullabies of sweetness and light which the neo-Freudians serve up as psycho-analysis.[3]

And yet it is precisely the pessimism in Freud which gives us the best hope.

It is one of the sad ironies of contemporary intellectual

[1] Brown, op. cit., p. 7. [2] Ibid., p. 16. [3] Ibid., p. 98.

life that Freud's hypothesis of an innate death instinct, which has been received with horror as the acme of pessimism, actually offers the only way out of the really pessimistic hypothesis of an innate aggressive instinct.[1]

Indeed, it is an indication of Freud's honesty that he should swing between pessimism and optimism: for the swing is due to the pull between 'his deep humanitarian desire to help mankind, and his intellectual realism, which refused to accept a cheap and easy solution'.[2] Freud taught, of course, that the chief aim of psycho-analytical healing is always to replace repression by sublimation; but he has to admit that not all of the *libido* can be sublimated, and therefore he cannot claim to be able to promise complete satisfaction in sublimation.

> One can sympathise [says Brown] with the neo-Freudians' desire to formulate psycho-analysis as a social science; in view of Freud's ambiguities, one can sympathise with their abandonment of the concept of sublimation. But the concept of sublimation is a command to relate the human spirit (and its creations) to the human body. In abandoning the concept, the neo-Freudians abandon the body, and then inevitably have to return to the autonomous spiritual concepts and norms traditional in Western culture and challenged by Freud. The concept of sublimation commands us to grasp social phenomena as pathological, in medical and scientific terms. When the neo-Freudians lose sight of the body they abandon the scientific criticism of society, and either preach social adjustment or else fall back on their own private prejudices in favour of the 'democratic personality' or the 'self-actualizing personality' or whatever.[3]

[1] Brown, op. cit., p. 99.
[2] Ibid., p. 57.
[3] Ibid., p. 144.

This is not the place to follow Dr Brown into his fascinating, if daunting, exploration down the drains and sewers of Western culture, his defence of (e.g.) Martin Luther's 'cloacal language', nor his poetic account of the Christian doctrine of the Resurrection of the Body as prefiguring Freudian truths. It is enough to have seen how he rescues some of Freud's obscure, and seemingly perverse, insights. When Freud suggests that man's superiority over the rest of the animal kingdom lies in his capacity for neurosis, he seems to be merely making a cynical-sounding joke. But when he goes on to show that man's capacity for neurosis is 'merely the obverse of his capacity for cultural development',[1] we wake with a start to find he has thrown a sudden new illumination upon a tired familiar landscape. When Freud states that religion is a 'substitute-gratification', he seems to be purely destructive. But when he adds that, so is poetry, and dreams and neurotic symptoms, and that therefore substitute-gratifications contain truth – 'they are expressions, distorted by repression, of the immortal desires of the human heart'[2] – we find we are getting somewhere. It may seem a little extreme to conclude from a study of Freud that:

> The decadence of Protestantism may be measured by the decline of diabolism and eschatology. Theologies (including later Lutheranism) which lack a real sense of the Devil lack Luther's capacity for critical detachment from the world, lack Luther's disposition to fight the Devil, and end by calling the Devil's work God's work . . . [And this leads

[1] Brown, op. cit., p. 10.
[2] Ibid., p. 13.

to the degeneration of the social doctrine of Lutheranism into] a religious sanction of the existing situation.[1]

But if indeed Dr Brown's reading of Freud is a fair one, the Freudian language which makes so much use of *dramatis personae* does suggest that a theology, as much as a humanism, which lacks a sense of real conflict is untrue to life. And if in addition we see Freud as the great leveller ('We are all somewhat hysterical'; the difference between so-called normality and neurosis is only 'a matter of degree'),[2] then his diagnosis of our ills is important for every one of us. And finally the modesty of his claims is in itself a measure of their authenticity. When he promised some kind of help to his patients, through use of his psycho-analytic therapy, they often (he tells us) challenged him about what he really could offer them.

I was often faced by this objection: 'Why, you tell me yourself that my illness is probably connected with my circumstances and the events of my life. You cannot alter these in any way. How do you propose to help me then?' And I have been able to make this reply: 'No doubt fate would find it easier than I do to relieve you of your illness. But you will be able to convince yourself that much will be gained if we succeed in transforming your hysterical misery into common unhappiness.'[3]

IV. *Dissent*

Such is the case for psycho-analysis – presented in the

[1] Brown, op. cit., p. 217.

[2] Freud, *Three Esssay* (Standard Edit. III/171); Analysis Terminable and interminable (*Collected Papers* V, p. 337): cited in Rieff, p. 354.

[3] Freud, *Studies in Hysteria* (Standard Edit. II/305): Rieff, p. 327.

terms of the man who was incomparably the most important psychological thinker of our time. But there are dissenters to it, not from the side of scientific psychology, but from that of the artist. But since Freud found such large room for man the rebel and man the misfit, let us listen to a rebel against psycho-analysis. The American novelist Norman Mailer was being questioned a little while ago, and was asked whether he thought that psycho-analysis had anything to say about the nature of the universe. He replied:

> I see it as an instrument of conformity. Psycho-analysts are sedentary middle-class people and I see no reason to give nature and the universe over to sedentary middle-class people. In America now there's a new establishment, what I call the establishment of the centre: people who are right-wing Socialists and left-wing – no, that's inaccurate, modern – Conservatives, who all work together. And their great handmaid is psycho-analysis. It's almost impossible for anyone to do anything individual without being crucified in those mediocre and dreary salons which pop up like mushrooms all over New York. I've seen the city dying over the last ten years. There's a psychic poverty in the city today, perhaps in the whole country. . . .[1]

There is one other piece of evidence worth quoting in the same vein, from a work of imaginative literature. In the strange powerful novel by the German novelist, Elias Canetti, *Auto-da-Fé*, the hero, Peter Kien, has a brother, George who is head of a large mental hospital. He had started as a doctor, but became interested in mental cases through coming across a madman who

[1] Norman Mailer, interview with R. Wollheim, *New Statesman*, 29th Sept., 1961.

composed his own language – a language in which objects have no special names but words are used for relations only: a language

hurled into the room like living tree trunks.[1]

George Kien became head of a hospital, and all of the 800 cases loved him. He effected many cures. But

When George walked along the streets of Paris it sometimes happened that he met one of his cures. He would be embraced and almost knocked down, like the master of some enormous dog coming home after a long absence. Under his friendly questions he concealed a timid hope. He . . . waited for just one such little comment as 'Then it was nicer!' or 'How empty and stupid my life is now!, I wish I were ill again!' 'Why did you cure me?' . . . (etc.).

Instead, compliments and invitations rained on him. His ex-patients looked plump, well and common. Their speech was in no way different from that of any passer-by. . . .

When they had still been his friends and guests, they were troubled with some gigantic guilt, which they carried for all, or with their littleness which stood in such ridiculous contrast to the hugeness of ordinary men, or with the idea of conquering the world, or with death – a thing which they now felt to be quite ordinary. Their riddles had flickered out; earlier they lived for riddles; now for things long ago solved. George was ashamed of himself. . . . He had been outwitted by his profession.[2]

What the neo-Freudians would say to this, or to Mr Mailer, I do not know; but I cannot think that Freud himself would have been disturbed by it: indeed, I fancy he would have enjoyed the joke.

[1] Elias Canetti, *Auto-da-Fé* (trs. V. Wedgwood; Cape, 1946), p. 402.

[2] Cannetti, pp. 404-5.

And this, perhaps, shows us the essential neutrality of the central core of psycho-analysis. A complete ethical neutrality is, of course, impossible; and Mr Rieff's book, used in the last section, certainly shows Freud as a 'moralist'. A complete metaphysical neutrality is also, no doubt, impossible: indeed where Freud's metaphysical positivism peeps through it is damaging to his case. But an area of deliberate neutrality is a practical necessity for anyone engaged in a pluralist world, and I believe that psycho-analysis in Freud's employment achieves this more often than not.

I can best explain this by citing evidence rather different from that which occurs in the usual case-book of analysts. The evidence is presented by a French Roman Catholic, formerly a Marxist and one who had no religious background whatever until he was twenty-seven. Ignace Lepp's book is called *Psychoanalyse de l'athéisme moderne*,[1] and has not been translated into English (at the time of writing). His background will no doubt make him suspect at once, so I hasten to quote the caveat with which he prefaces his cases. First he says that there is an atheism which is neurotic in origin – this is the theme of his book; but there are, he insists, plenty of non-neurotic atheists: and, again, a man may be neurotic without his atheism – or his faith – being affected.

> To avoid any pseudo-apologetic exploitation of them [the cases to be discussed] let us remember that there are also believers whose faith bears clearly the stigmata of neurosis.

[1] Ignace Lepp, *Psychoanalyse de l'athéisme moderne* (Grasset, 1961).

Besides, in many of their manifestations neurotic belief and unbelief are very like each other, much more like each other than neurotic belief resembles authentic faith, or neurotic atheism resembles healthy unbelief.[1]

Here, then, are two of the cases with which he dealt in his psycho-analytic practice (true cases – though the names, and recognizable circumstances, have of course been altered). I summarize them, rather than giving lengthy quotations from M. Lepp's book.

First, we have the curious case of Irma, who specialized in seducing priests, especially pious ones, whom she would then delate to the bishop. She boasted that she had got two unfrocked, and ruined the reputation of about ten others. She actually came to the psychotherapist for quite other reasons.

It emerged that her parents were fairly conventionally atheistic. At university she had met a young priest, chaplain to the students. She became a fervent Catholic, and even converted her parents. She had long spiritual conversations with the chaplain, and he taught her the practice of divine love, and other devout exercises. Finally he suggested that she ought to test her vocation to the Contemplative Life. At first she was horrified – for this would mean her separation from him; but then she came to see it as a chance for a supreme sacrifice. Her family opposed it, but she entered an order, and started to practise extreme mortifications. Indeed, she tried to outdo the rest in austerity. On the eve of her clothing as a novice she wrote to the priest that she was

[1] Lepp, op. cit., p. 52.

about to make the final sacrifice – her hair. After she had taken the habit, all began to go badly. She became melancholy, depressed, and was constantly weeping. She redoubled her mortifications, until she became ill. The Superior then wisely decided to send her back into 'the world'. Proud of her ascetic practices, she resisted this: she believed herself to be the victim of persecution by the mediocre and luke-warm majority in the convent. She had almost to be pushed out of the convent: and she left, without any farewells, and with hatred in her heart.

How could she return to her parents – they had opposed her entry in the first place? In spite of (or because of!) her rough penances, she was now more beautiful than when she entered the convent. As she waited for a bus, a stranger spoke to her. In a few minutes, without looking at him, she went into a café with him for a drink – and then, with complete apathy, to a hotel bedroom. After that she felt she could face her parents: she had faced the depths of cynicism. The next Saturday, out of habit, she went to confession. The priest, who (like her chaplain friend) was young and pious, questioned her closely about her sin, and seemed shocked that a former religious should fall into 'mortal sin' so easily. He admonished her severely. Irma felt no remorse: on the contrary, she merely felt that he hadn't sympathized with her state of distress, as she had left the convent. Her first thought was 'I wish you were in my place, then you'd understand'. And then the idea came to her to put him in that place. She feigned deep penitence, and asked for more direction. She went to his room for spiritual help – and in a few weeks, to her own surprise, she became his mistress. Soon she delated him to the bishop, and was delighted when he was packed off to the Trappists.

It became clear in the course of the analysis that she identified all these priest-victims with her first director (the young chaplain). She said: 'If only he, instead of sending her to the convent, could have had the courage to love me as a man does a woman, I should never have known this moral collapse and loss of faith.' M. Lepp's concluding comment is:

> It took many months for her to achieve reconciliation with herself and then with others. Only after that did her atheism cease to be aggressive and neurotic. I lost touch with her after her recovery, and don't know whether she's still an unbeliever or has recovered her faith. If the latter, it's very likely that her religious life will be quite unlike the exalted mysticism she practised before. And if she's still stuck in unbelief, it'll be a serene unbelief.[1]

The other case I shall quote is that of Oscar. He was an unbeliever, but married a young Catholic girl – religion was indifferent to him. But her parents insisted that he should be baptized first. For this he had to have some instruction: but the priest was very busy, and only gave him four or five lessons in the catechism, and told him he must carry on, by reading, afterwards. All this meant nothing to him; but being of a tolerant nature, he let his children be brought up Christian, and sometimes even accompanied his wife to mass. It seemed to be an ideal, settled kind of 'mixed marriage'.

[1] Lepp, op. cit., pp. 67-8.

But suddenly he began to be obsessed with the idea of death. He saw it everywhere; he tried to avoid meeting it, yet it always seemed to be there, staring at him, in the pages of the newspapers he happened to be reading. From being a tolerant agnostic, he became a bitter atheist; he began to practise freemasonry, deliberately; and also to suffer from insomnia.

Under analysis it became clear that, without knowing it, he had been disquieted from his very first contacts with his wife. He had said he would not exert any pressure on her, but he was insistent that she must not exert any on him either. Lepp explains:

His atheist super-ego was of an extreme rigidity: he repressed the latent interest in religion before it could reach the level of consciousness. But what happened to him was, in reaction, exactly what Freud describes with regard to the repression of the sexual impulse under the repressive power of the religious or moral super-ego. Repressed into the unconscious, his metaphysical disquietude became anarchical, and made its way to the level of consciousness, disguised as an anxiety, an anguish about death. . . . The more he struggled, the worse it became.

The psychotherapist advised him that he must boldly look at the religious problem straight in the face. In his case, he did study the Catholic faith, and later became a believer.[1]

But Lepp repeats his warning. We mustn't, he says, draw the conclusion that the psychotherapy of every anguished atheist must necessarily lead to acceptance of religious faith. Oscar's obsession might have ceased just

[1] Lepp, op. cit., p. 74.

as well if, after a study of the Christian faith, he had decided to reject the Christian message.

The cause of his trouble was not in fact his refusal to believe, but rather the unconscious nature of this refusal. It is not within the power of depth psychology to give, or to destroy, faith: the latter belongs to the metaphysical realm which theology calls *grace*.

I hope that anyone, whatever his views, would salute this demonstration of impartiality and objectivity on the part of a Christian analyst. It is interesting (if not, perhaps, wholly fair) to compare this with the attitude of a self-declared secular humanist psychologist, Professor J. C. Flügel. In a book first published in 1945, and twice reprinted (without alteration) he discusses the psycho-social effects of religion, and says that

> alongside of its beneficent functions, religion in its cruder forms can exercise a severe crippling and inhibiting effect upon the human mind, by fostering irrational anxiety and guilt, and by hampering the free play of the intellect.

And he concludes, unambiguously, that

> in the long run even an increase in individual neurosis may not be too high a price to pay for the removal of the restrictions it imposes.[1]

One cannot help wondering whether this confidant dogmatism about the 'reality principle' does not conceal a rather strenuous and even ruthless proselytizing determinism which is singularly absent from the Christian practitioner.

[1] J. C. Flügel, *Man, Morals and Society* (Kegan Paul, 1945), p. 271: (Penguin, 1962), p. 330.

Man the Rebel

I have said that there is a kind of neutrality at the central core of psycho-analysis: but one thing the psycho-analyst cannot be neutral about is psychic truth. The validity of the protest (Norman Mailer's or Elias Canetti's) against psycho-analysis itself, as aiming at a psychic conformism, parallel to a social conformism, depends on whether the protest is based on a true statement: is this conformism what psycho-analysts and psychiatrists induce in their patients? It is significant that the protest comes from the artist: and so to the artist we must turn. But it is only fair to acknowledge that Freud, at least, would have allowed – indeed, urged – us to do so. However unappreciative of music he may have been, he valued the creative writer: he often referred to art as a way of making the unconscious conscious. At the celebrations for his seventieth birthday, Freud was hailed by someone as 'the discoverer of the unconscious'. He at once disclaimed the distinction, in a famous phrase:

> The poets and philosophers before me discovered the unconscious; what I discovered was the scientific method by which the unconscious can be studied.[1]

D. H. Lawrence put it cogently: 'Never trust the artist. Trust the tale.'[2] For the work of art can belie the conscious convictions of its creator, as well as show up the falsities of the age. Works of art at their greatest are the lie-detectors of a culture. To them, therefore, we turn.

[1] Cited in N. O. Brown, op. cit., p. 62.

[2] D. H. Lawrence, 'The Spirit of Place' in *Selected Literary Criticism*, ed. A. Beal (Heinemann, 1956), p. 297.

6

The Lie-Detectors

›››◆‹‹‹

I. *The Artist as Seismologist*

THE function of the poet – and generally speaking, of the creator of values – is to disclose the fatal sickness of his epoch long before it declares itself openly, to unmask, beneath equivocal symptoms, the underlying corruption of energy, and to prevent the latter from flourishing blindly . . . to divert it from the seductive appeal of anarchy, and from that morbid exuberance which one sees in decaying organisms. . . . And, on the contrary, to bring it back to its centre, in man collected, reassured, reinvigorated by his limits.[1]

In any age the artist is one who advances through the night with sensitive antennae. He is the first to feel the long coils of bramble in the forest, the trip-wire or the hidden pit covered with brush-wood. He is the seismograph, recording the shock of the distant earthquake, which will be on its way to us next. He is the EEG of society, detecting its lies and evasions. He is, in Virgil Gheorghiu's phrase, the white rabbit in the submarine. In Gheorghiu's novel, *La Vingt-Cinquième Heure*, the hero, himself a novelist, describes how

I once went on a cruise in a submarine. I stayed under water for about forty-five days. In submarines there is a

[1] Pierre Emmanuel, *The Universal Singular* (Engl. tr.; Grey Walls Press, 1951), pp. 107-8.

special apparatus for indicating the exact moment when the air has to be renewed. But a long time ago there was no such apparatus, and the sailors took white rabbits on board instead. The moment the atmosphere became poisonous the rabbits died, and the sailors knew then that they had only five or six hours more to live. . . . In the submarine I went in there were no white rabbits, but there were detectors. The captain noticed that I could sense every diminution of the quantity of oxygen. At first he pooh-poohed my sensitiveness, but in the end he did not use the detectors: he only had to look at me. . . . It is a gift which we have – the white rabbits and I – to feel six hours before the rest of human beings the moment when the atmosphere becomes unbreathable.[1]

Or finally, the artist is, in the phrase of the French poet, Pierre Emmanuel, with which this chapter opens, the diagnostician of man's sickness.

Of course these analogies are not to be taken in too literal a sense, as if the function of every novelist was to be a fortune-teller and every poem an astrological chart. When that does happen – and it does happen from time to time, as in George Orwell's brilliant but hysterical *Nineteen-Eighty-Four*, in some of Mr Aldous Huxley's novels, such as *Ape and Essence* or and indeed in parts of Gheorghiu's novel quoted from above – then the artist becomes a pamphleteer. Again, it is not to be thought that the artist will produce a 'solution' to the problems he senses. When he does try to do so he often talks nonsense. As the Marxist literary critic, George Lukacs

[1] C. Virgil Gheorghiu, *La Vingt-Cinquième Heure* (Plon, 1949), p. 117.

(whom I shall discuss in the last section of this chapter), says, of understanding the dialectic of historical development:

> Only 'prophetic' vision, or subsequent study of a completed period, can grasp the unity underlying sharp contradictions. One would be misunderstanding the role of perspective in literature, though, if one were to identify 'prophetic' understanding with correct political foresight. If such foresight were the criterion, there would have been no successful typology in nineteenth-century literature. For it was precisely the greatest writers of that age – Balzac and Stendhal, Dickens and Tolstoy – who erred most in their view of what the future would be like. Yet it was not accident that made possible the creation of typical, universal characters in their work.[1]

It is interesting that a Marxist writer should use the word 'prophet' in its traditional sense: this was, indeed, what the ancient prophet did, and the roles of poet and prophet are still related as they have been from early times.[2] The serious arts register changes in the barometric pressure of thought and life sooner and more sensitively than most.

The serious artist. Because, of course, not any old artist will do. And it is one of the functions of the literary critic to judge who is 'serious' and who is not. How is this done? Largely by examining his language. This does not merely mean his technique. You can, and must, examine the way a painter lays on his paint, how he

[1] George Lukacs, *The Meaning of Contemporary Realism*, 1957 (Engl. tr.; Merlin Press, 1963), p. 56.

[2] Nora K. Chadwick, *Poetry and Prophecy* (C.U.P., 1942).

uses his brush, and so forth; but to examine the total effect, to which the technique contributes, is also to examine an operation. So, in the case of the poet, with words. F. W. Bateson puts it:

> A society's effective life can be measured in economic and political terms, but the history of the language provides a more sensitive index to the births and deaths of the dominant groups.[1]

For instance (he says), the date 1650 is a watershed: it marks the end of an inflationary period, the degradation of monarchy, the abolition of feudal tenures, the end of centralized government, colonial expansion and the struggle against the Dutch navy, religious and racial toleration, the foundation of the later 'Royal Society', and the trend towards scientific agriculture. Each of these by itself looks as if it might have been accidental. 'But where politics and economics offer only tentative approximations, the linguistic evidence is decisive.' And he takes as a specimen for examination the word 'romance', which occurs suddenly for the first time as an adjective in no less than seven writers between the years 1650 and 1659.

It is possible indeed, to exaggerate the relationship between art and society. Mr Bateson says:

> To understand a poem's meaning today we need to be able to identify ourselves as far as possible with its original readers . . . whose ideal response to the poem in fact constitutes its meaning.

[1] F. W. Bateson, *English Poetry: A Critical Introduction* (Longmans, 1950), pp. 94-6.

But he also says:

> The subject-matter of poetry is not 'things', but conflicting moods and attitudes, human nature *in its social relations*.[1]

This can be taken to dangerous lengths. When the late Professor H. J. Laski learned that Mr T. S. Eliot had announced himself a Christian, he wrote:

> When the poet ceases to be Shelley's 'unacknowledged legislator of the world' it is because he has ceased to find meaning in the world . . . it is rather the echo of his own voice than the message he has to proclaim that is of importance to him. . . . He thus deliberately turns his back upon the supreme issue of whether it is in our power to elevate the standards of value and taste throughout our society. . . . Great literature cannot be either a means of escape merely from the tragic burden of life, nor can it seek to provide the artist with no more than a means of self-realisation.

And he puts Mr Eliot among those who

> desert the main task to which they are called . . . of giving their fellow citizens counsel on the vital issues they have to solve.[2]

But this is precisely to expect art to become propaganda; indeed, Professor Laski's gravamen against Mr Eliot is curious, for many of Mr Eliot's critics have, on the contrary, accused him of declining from poet to Christian propagandist. And certainly the most thorough-going attempts to harness art to a social-humanist message

[1] Bateson, pp. 78, 100.

[2] H. J. Laski, *Faith, Reason and Civilisation* (Gollancz, 1944), pp. 109, 138: cited in D. E. S. Maxwell, *The Poetry of T. S. Eliot* (Routledge, 1952), p. 122.

(those in the U.S.S.R.) do not encourage us to hope great things for 'proletarian art'. As the late editor of *Esprit*, Emmanuel Mounier, once remarked:

> To hand over the art of today to the judgement of the masses, before a new and true community has been constructed, is to hand over not to what one admires in the masses, but to those of their reflexes which have become bourgeois.[1]

The alternate thaws and freezes in Russia, the blooming and withering of the hundred flowers in China, only go to show that the arts constantly fight back against any attempt to keep them in a purely political strait-jacket.

Opposite the Scylla of Marxist despotism lies the Charybdis of psychotherapy. By this I mean the tendency to regard the arts simply from the pragmatic, social point of view, as a form of occupational therapy. Sir Herbert Read is not to blame if the theme of his book, *Education Through Art*, may have led to an over-emphasis upon this aspect. Of course we do not decry the interesting and sometimes moving exhibitions of paintings by subnormal children, epileptics, psychotics, etc. Certainly art is therapeutic. (So is prayer.) But a painting looked at or executed *solely* for the sake of coping with a manic-depressive phase is not likely to be very good painting: any more than a prayer offered merely to escape spiritual aridity is likely to effect this end. When we are given (as we have been from time to time) a detailed and technical examination of, say, *Hamlet* (man and play) we may be getting something useful; we may

[1] Quoted in G. Severini, *The Artist and Society* (Harvill, 1946), p. 23.

be gaining professional confirmation for what we knew intuitively all along – that Shakespeare was, among other things, a brilliant psychologist. But if it is thereby suggested that this is to be the touchstone of Shakespeare's genius, then we see that psychology has intruded beyond its own sphere. Indeed, what the psychological critic does not usually realize is that a play like *Hamlet*, which provides him with such excellent material for his own technique, may often be a less great play the better its psychology is done – precisely because a great drama must be more than an accurate case-history.

This is not to say that there is (e.g.) no sexual symbolism in literature, nor that elucidation of it is not sometimes valuable for the understanding of writers and painters. But to reduce all literary criticism to psychological detection is to fail as a critic.

What can be said is that the artist is an uncoverer of the roots of society. M. Jean-Paul Sartre may be right when he says that one reason for the defects of nineteenth-century as compared with eighteenth-century writers is this: that in the eighteenth century they wrote both for the men of the old order, which they were at the same time undermining, and for the new order, the rising bourgeoisie, whose hopes and aspirations they expressed; whereas the writers of the nineteenth century sneered at the bourgeoisie and yet could not shake themselves free from it. But Sartre is not therefore necessarily also right to conclude that the contemporary writer ('*la littérature engagée*') must work for a society in which democratic socialism is achieving an equality of classes so that his 'ideal' public shall not be distinct from his 'real' public.[1] What is really to the point, in the artist's relations to society, is the cohesion rather than the levelling-out of that society. And here the beliefs (religious or otherwise) of the people in the society are important. It can be contended that a society without belief is not a society but an agglomeration: not a 'home', in which all the bits and pieces take on an air of 'belonging' there, but a furniture-store.

Here I think another of the arts, music, can be a useful barometer. In a fascinating study of English music over the past four to five hundred years,[2] Mr Wilfred Mellers constantly refers to the part played by society in the preservation and development of our musical tradition. He reckons that:

> The sixteenth century, which the nineteenth century considered rhythmically 'vague', actually developed rhythm to the highest point it has reached in European history, and perhaps it is no accident that in England this supreme musical rhythmic development coincides with the development of mature Shakespearean blank verse, with its parallel reconciliation of speech rhythm with metrical accent.[3]

And he quotes the judgement of Tovey, that the 'purists' in the sixteenth century

> . . . were the men of far-sighted musical intellect, and in general it was the inaccurate artists that were dull. In no other period has the criterion of 'correctness' been so

[1] J.-P. Sartre, *What is Literature?* (*Situations* II) (Engl. tr.; Methuen, 1950).
[2] Wilfred Mellers, *Music and Society* (Dobson, 1946, 1950).
[3] Ibid., p. 50.

closely equated with the opinion and practice of genius, and, of course, this could be so only because . . . music really was a social and religious manifestation. . . .

In England [in the late seventeenth century] the Christian humanist tradition turned sour; . . . we fell pitifully between the 'protestant' and the 'aristocratic' stools. . . . [For all the Puritans' fondness for music] the disapproval of the Puritans combined with the decline of the aristocracy to bring about the submergence of the masque, which was the point from which Lully had started, so that the art of Ben Jonson, at once courtly and popular, was not assimilated into the new theatrical tradition. . . .[1]

And what happened in the end was that we got the death of the musical tradition, the death-blow being administered by the Oratorio.

The idea of sitting solemnly in rows and listening to music 'for its own sake' would have seemed absurd to Byrd or Palestrina; either one made music oneself or one listened to it as homage to God. . . . Music for [Byrd] was an *activity*; he did not think of it primarily as a means of expressing the state of his soul (though it was such unavoidably).

With the decay of any sense of music's 'moral' significance – its significance in terms of human life – it isn't surprising that when Handel brought the Italian opera to England the English tradition, what was left of it, should have been totally unable to assimilate it. . . . Handel, as a foreigner, could not himself help English composers to incorporate the new theatre music into their own . . . Handel was a business man. . . . Handel had to deal with a rising middle-class public which was mainly passive and trained, not on a dramatic tradition, but on the realistic novel. . . . [He] made little or no attempt to achieve inflectional subtlety in

[1] Mellers, op. cit., pp. 57, 79-81.

his line or to achieve any organic relation between that line and the English language . . . but he produced an idiom exactly suited to the temper of the era of the Roast Beef of Old England and imperialist expansion. It was done with superb genius of course: but it finally polished off what little was left of the native tradition.[1]

Even if other critics should dissent from some of these judgements, it remains true that the musicologist has something deeply significant to say about the society in which music is being produced and appreciated, and that means about man's responses within that society.

II. *The Artist Against Society*

But this is to see the artist on the whole as 'in tune with' society. Surely the most common and representative picture we have of him is as the more or less professional anarchist? It is this that has made the late Albert Camus so much the hero and saint of modern literature – for though we can admire Sartre's agility of mind we can't, surely, be ever profoundly moved by his novels and plays, whereas in Camus we find a genuine creative and poetic imagination. And there is something in his reading of man's situation today which makes him particularly sympathetic to the intellectual of our time.

Pessimiste quant à la destinée humaine, je suis optimiste quant à l'homme.[2]

And when he applies this more specifically to 'rebel man'

[1] Mellers, op. cit., pp. 91, 95-6.

[2] Albert Camus, *Actuelles. Chroniques*, 1944-8 (Gallimard, 1950), pp. 325f.

(*l'homme révolté*) he seems to voice the feelings of many a poet and novelist in the West.

> No wisdom can give us anything more than this. *La révolte* tirelessly butts its head against evil. . . . Man must repair by his creations all that can be repaired. After which, children will still go on dying unjustly, even in a perfect society. In his greatest effort, man can only set himself deliberately to diminish arithmetically the pain in the world. . . .

The English edition of *L'Homme Révolté* omitted the epigraph from Hölderlin which Camus has in the original:

> Openly I dedicated myself to the grave and suffering earth; and often, in the sacred night, I promised to love it, with its heavy burden of fatality, faithfully and without fear, and to scorn none of its enigmas.

And Camus cannot forget the agonized cry of Dmitri Karamazov, in *The Brothers Karamazov*, over the death of a child:

> Rebellion cannot exist without a strange form of love. Those who find no rest in God or in history are condemned to live for those who, like themselves, cannot live . . . for the humiliated. The most pure form of the movement of rebellion is thus crowned with the heart-rending cry of Karamazov: if all are not saved, what good is the salvation of one only?

Absolute faith in a political mode of salvation is no answer:

> Contemporary materialism . . . believes that it can answer all questions. But, as a slave to history, it increases the domain

of historic murder and at the same time leaves it without any justification, except in the future – which again demands faith. In both cases one must wait and, meanwhile, the innocent continue to die. For twenty centuries the sum-total of evil has not diminished in the world. No paradise, whether divine or revolutionary, has been realized. An injustice remains inextricably bound to all suffering, even the most deserved in the eyes of men. . . .

Men of 'revolt' must

refuse . . . to be deified in that they reject the unlimited power to inflict death. They choose, and we offer as an example, the only original rule of life to-day: to learn to live and to die, and in order to be a man, to refuse to be a god.

And finally:

There does exist, therefore, a way of acting and of thinking, for man, which are possible of the level of moderation to which he belongs. Every undertaking which is more ambitious than this proves to be contradictory. The absolute is not attained, nor above all, created, through history. Politics is not religion, or, if it is, then it is nothing but the Inquisition. How would society define an absolute? . . . Society and politics only have the responsibility of arranging everyone's affairs so that each will have the leisure and the freedom to pursue this common search. History can then no longer be presented as an object of worship. . . . It is those who know how to rebel, at the appropriate moment, against history who really advance its interests.[1]

Something like this mood can be found in a very wide variety of English, and some American, novelists today.

[1] Albert Camus, *L'Homme Révolté* (Gallimard, 1951): Eng. trs. by A. Bower, *The Rebel* (Hamilton, 1959), pp. 271, 270-71, 273, 269.

It is difficult to give examples, first because the writers are so varied, and second because so few of the post-Thomas Mann generation of novelists (and dramatists) are of any literary stature. It is hard to escape the feeling that those who most clearly echo the 'classical pessimism' and modest humanism of Camus are trying to reproduce in times of peace a mood created during or around the last war: a rather febrile attempt to find a 'they' equivalent to the Nazis to protest against. And as the indignation of the 'Angries' seems to have found an inadequate object, the quality of their compassion, too, seems to suffer. Camus' notion of 'the absurd' is attractive in a society which has lost its roots in any kind of tradition – but unless it is 'worked for' as hard as Camus worked, it can represent a very arbitrary kind of anarchism.

There can be, certainly, a passionate conviction based largely on a rejection of extremes. In that quietly impressive novel of Lionel Trilling's, *The Middle of the Journey*, there is a conversation between the Marxist, Gifford Maxim, the Christians, Nancy and Arthur Croome, and the unattached liberal, John Laskell. Gifford Maxim explains how the two parties of dogma need for the moment to make a pact: he says:

I'm sorry – but we [Marxists and Christians] must go hand in hand. . . . We will hate each other and we will make the new world. And when we've made it, and it has done its work, then maybe we will resurrect John Laskell (*sc.* the liberal). Remember it! [– pointing to John Laskell –] It is the last time you will see it. . . . The supreme act of the humanistic critical intelligence – it perceives the cogency of the argument, and acquiesces in the fact of its own extinction.[1]

'You are wrong on one point [said Laskell]. I do not acquiesce.'

[Maxim:] Of course . . . you could not possibly acquiesce. But it does not matter, John, whether you do or not.

'It matters', Laskell said. 'Oh it matters very much. It is the only thing that matters.'[2]

But this is not, I think, characteristic of the mood of writers of the 'fifties and 'sixties. It is perhaps closer to that of Thomas Mann.

Thomas Mann once discussed 'religion'.

Religion! Yes, I once heard the literary champion of civilization hold forth on religion. It was at the graveside of a poet of whom it was said that his last hours had been filled with religious scruples. He had cried out for God and perhaps died believing in Him. How did this *Zivilisationsliterat* set about apologizing on his behalf, how did he solve his own embarrassment? 'Our duty towards the spirit,' he said '*which we call religion*', – of that duty the deceased had been most vividly aware. Well, we know what the *Zivilisationsliterat* means when he says 'spirit'. He means literature, he means politics, he means both together, namely Democracy. And that he calls religion! When I heard these solemnities of a counterfeiter of ideas, of a 'liberally religious' Sunday preacher who claimed for that sort of 'spirit' a soul which in its extremity had longed for salvation – when I heard it, I put on my hat and went home.[3]

[1] For Laskell had just contradicted Nancy by saying that Maxim was not mad.

[2] Lionel Trilling, *The Middle of the Journey* (Secker, 1948), p. 323.

[3] T. Mann: cited in Erich Heller, *The Ironic German* (Secker, 1958), p. 142.

And Mann goes on to ask whether the 'literary champion of civilization', with his concern for social re-arrangement, does not conjure up the deplorable prospect of a 'morally castrated life', a life 'robbed of all its tragic accents? . . . Is not doubt more religious than belief – the belief in the virtuous society?' All this is a distasteful substitute for true belief. But what, then, is true belief?

> 'It is the belief in God.' 'Yet what is God? Is it not the comprehensive vision, the principle of form, the omniscient justice, the love affirming everything that is? . . . Belief in God is the belief in love, in life, and in art. . . .'
>
> 'I cannot say that I believe in God, and even if I did believe, it would be a long time before I said so.' Doubt is better than false belief – 'and despair is a more religious condition than the mellifluous religiosity of the revolutionary optimist.'[1]

This kind of honesty and poise lies behind the great series of novels Mann produced. Eric Heller sums up that achievement in these words:

> Thomas Mann was one of the few writers who, by giving valid form to the chaotic mind of this century, will have helped it to be remembered with at least a measure of friendliness and respect.[2]

So far I have quoted almost exclusively, not from poems, plays or novels, but from the reflective and theoretical compositions of men who are novelists, dramatists, etc. And this is dangerous: for it is only as engaged in the actual creative imaginative work that these men either speak true or have any special claim,

[1] T. Mann: Heller, pp. 147-8. [2] Heller, p. 285.

over any other theorists, to be listened to. The excuse for using the former rather than the latter must be one of space. It requires a book, or indeed several books, to show the varied contributions of twentieth-century writers through their understandings of man: Lawrence showing up the death of man through 'mentalizing' processes that should be instinctive and 'quick'; Yeats showing man as a myth-surrounded being advancing through tangled thickets of hatred; Kafka showing man hopelessly outnumbered by the forces of intimidation and efficiency yet obstinately picking himself up and walking on; Camus showing the absurdity of existence which only calls out the stronger for man's defiance; Thomas Mann showing the power of irony to hold back the inevitable advances of chaos over tradition . . . and so forth. And there could be, too, a revealing study of influences, a pedigree of literary themes. Most of them would reach back sooner or later to Dostoevsky. For instance, the famous cry of Dmitri Karamazov, in which he rejects 'the harmony' of the universe because the death of one innocent child is enough to shatter it ('It's not God that I don't accept, Alyosha, only I most respectfully return Him the ticket'[1]) is taken up by Thomas Mann as well as Camus. In Mann's great novel, *Doktor Faustus*, it is the agonizing death of Adrian Leverkühn's little nephew that finally drives the composer hero to the extremities of his nihilistic music. And Camus, whom we have already seen quoting Dmitri Karamazov in *L'Homme Révolté*, repeats the theme in the

[1] Dostoevsky, *The Brothers Karamazov* (Heinemann), p. 317.

crucial scene of *La Peste*, when the screams of the small child dying of the plague set Dr Rieux and Père Paneloux arguing about the range of their possible co-operation (the priest helping the doctor) in the work of 'healing'. There is another line of pedigree, less well-known, that runs from Dostoevsky's tale 'The Dream of a Ridiculous Man', into Camus and Simone de Beauvoir. In Dostoevsky's story a man is in despair about life, and is on his way home to shoot himself. A little girl runs up to him, as he walks home, and begs him to come at once – her mother is dying. He brushes her off and goes on home. But that night he is filled with remorse: he could have helped the little girl – why didn't he? And all night his remorse gives him nightmares. But next morning he realizes he has not kept his intention – to kill himself. And he sees, paradoxically, that it is his sin of neglect that has kept him alive: it is the remorse that awakens in him the realization that some things *do* matter – and it was because he had thought that nothing matters that he had intended to take his own life.[1] In Mme Simone de Beauvoir's *Les Mandarins* the heroine, Anne, during a time of deep depression, neglects her little girl, Maria, who is ill. Once again, it is the realization of her neglect that pulls her out of her near-suicidal mood.[2] And finally, in Albert Camus' last little 'tale' – which some critics consider to be, along with *L'Étranger*, his best – *La Chute*, the 'judge-penitent', Clamard, gradually reveals over the café table that he has failed

[1] Dostoevsky, *The Diary of a Writer* (Cassell, 1951) II, pp. 672ff.
[2] S. de Beauvoir, *Les Mandarins* (Gallimard, 1955).

to rescue a little girl who had fallen into the canal: and it is his almost gloating penitence over this that gives his 'absurd' life some significance.[1] These are just a few of the possible ways in which men – Christian or secular-humanist – can find illumination upon problems of human living.

III. *The Artist as Artist*

But this is still too general and abstract. For, as we have insisted in section one, it is the language that counts, *le style, c'est l'homme*. So that a proper use of contemporary literature must look at it in detail, comparing, not so much theme with theme as words with words. One example must suffice to show how important this is. In his *The Picaresque Saint*, a useful study of five post-'thirties novelists (Moravia, Camus, Silone, Faulkner and Graham Greene), Mr R. W. B. Lewis points out that the staccato style in which Camus' *L'Étranger* is written expresses perfectly the character of its 'hero', Mersault.

There is no discernible causal relation: the concept of cause no longer pushes perceptions into a usable order; Mersault's favourite conjunction is the colorless 'and' – never 'since', 'because' or 'therefore'. . . . The only passage in the novel where causal relations are asserted is the speech for the prosecution at Mersault's trial. The presence of such relations is one reason why Mersault feels that the speech is about someone else, not about himself.[2]

[1] Albert Camus, *La Chute* (Gallimard, 1956): Engl. trs., *The Fall* (Hamilton, 1957).

[2] R. W. B. Lewis, *The Picaresque Saint* (Gollancz, 1960), pp. 69, 300.

This is brilliantly observed: and it takes us at once to the heart of an important question about contemporary literature. Camus' Mersault is a rootless, disconnected, tragic perhaps but essentially 'decadent' figure. Is literature about decadents itself decadent literature? This is not a rhetorical question, for one literary critic of considerable power has in effect answered 'Yes' to it. I have already alluded to Mr George Lukacs, the Hungarian Marxist, whose independence of mind has led to his being more than once out of favour with the communist authorities in Eastern Europe. Some years back he wrote what seemed then a rather doctrinaire book of literary criticism, *Studies in European Realism*. But his more recent *The Meaning of Contemporary Realism* is a work of remarkable objectivity and penetration. He divides European literature of the twentieth century into three main blocks. There is what he calls 'Modernism', the dominant trend in the West, represented by writers like Kafka, Joyce, Musil, Gide, Eliot, Virginia Woolf, Lawrence, Faulkner and Samuel Beckett. Then there is 'Social Realism', i.e. Marxist literary writing. And finally there is 'Critical Realism', represented by (above all) Conrad and Thomas Mann, but also lesser writers like Rolland, Shaw, Dreiser and even Thomas Wolfe.

Lukacs' contention is that the first type of tradition, Modernism, is in the long run barren. For it leads (Musil is a good example, and Virginia Woolf is perhaps the most extreme example) to the dissolution of personality. The 'stream of consciousness', along with the monologue, becomes not merely a useful technique for revealing a character's thoughts, but the essential representation of the characters themselves. And this is because behind them lies the influence of Freud and the consequent centrality of the pathological. Kafka presents the crucial case here: for Lukacs acknowledges that Kafka was one of the greatest realistic writers of all time – and

Never was the quality of Kafka's achievement more striking or more needed than at the present day, when so many writers fall for slick experimentation. The impact of Kafka's work derives not only from his passionate sincerity – rare enough in our age – but also from the corresponding simplicity of the world he constructs. That is Kafka's most original achievement.[1]

And Kafka is marvellous, says Lukacs, for his representative quality: his

Vision of a world dominated by *angst* and of man at the mercy of incomprehensible terrors, makes Kafka's work the very type of modernist art . . . Kafka's *angst* is the experience *par excellence* of modernism.

But by using the allegorical method, he allows details to be 'annihilated by his transcendental Nothingness'; and this bars his way to realism.

Kafka is not able, in spite of his extraordinary evocative power, in spite of his unique sensibility, to achieve that fusion of the particular and the general which is the essence of realistic art.[2]

[1] G. Lukacs, *The Meaning of Contemporary Realism*, p. 77.
[2] Ibid., pp. 45-6.

And so in spite of his genius, his influence is baneful. For

> Modernism leads not only to the destruction of traditional literary forms; it leads to the destruction of literature as such. And this is true not only of Joyce, or of the literature of Expressionism and Surrealism. It was not André Gide's ambition, for instance, to bring about a revolution in literary style; it was his philosophy that compelled him to abandon conventional forms. He planned his *Faux-Monnayeurs* as a novel. But its structure suffered from a characteristically modernist schizophrenia: it was supposed to be written by the man who was also the hero of the novel. And, in practice, Gide was forced to admit that no novel, no work of literature could be constructed in that way. We have here a practical demonstration that . . . modernism means not the enrichment, but the negation of art.[1]

One might expect this demolition of 'modernism' to lead to a nice, conventional Marxist conclusion that only the second of Lukacs' three traditions – socialist realism – can provide healthy literature today. But Lukacs is much too good a critic to say this. He does, indeed, believe that socialism is the only possible goal ahead, and therefore socialist realism is historically speaking, superior to all else, because of 'the insights which socialist ideology, socialist perspective, make available to the writer: they enable him to give a more comprehensive and deeper account of man as a social being than any traditional ideology.' But he emphasizes that 'this superiority does not confer automatic success on each individual work of socialist realism'. And his

[1] Lukacs, op. cit., pp. 45-6.

critical discussion of this second group of writers is largely devoted to uncovering their woodenness, lack of imagination, and arid dogmatism. It is rather to the third group, what he regards as the great tradition of European realism, that he turns for hope. And when he says we have to choose between 'Franz Kafka or Thomas Mann?' (the title of his second chapter), he is claiming that Mann stands in the pedigree of Shakespeare, Stendhal, Balzac, Tolstoy, Dickens, and the rest. Take one example of the superiority of this 'critical realist tradition' to 'modernism': the treatment of time. The modernist regards experience of time as purely subjective. The realist writer, like Mann, is aware that this is true for certain classes of people; so he can employ the same kind of techniques as the modernist to describe the passage of time – but only for certain of his figures, whereas the modernist implies that this subjective experience constitutes reality as such.

Again and again Thomas Mann places characters with a time-experience of this subjectivist kind in relation to characters whose experience of time is normal and objective. In *The Magic Mountain* Hans Castorp represents the former type; Joachim Ziemssen and Hofrat Behrens the latter. Ziemssen is aware that this experience of time may be a result of living in a sanatorium, hermetically sealed off from everyday life. We arrive, therefore, at an important distinction: the modernist writer identifies what is necessarily a subjective experience with reality as such, thus giving a distorted picture of reality as a whole. (Virginia Woolf is an extreme example of this.) The realist, with his critical detachment, places what is a significant, specifically modern experience in a wider context, giving it only the emphasis it deserves as part of a greater, objective whole.[1]

And Lukacs also uses the notion of 'perspective' as that which is needed to give a depth to naturalistic description. For instance, he points to the 'reduction of human personality' in Camus (especially in *La Peste*):

> However suggestive as an allegory of the *condition humaine*, and however subtle the moral problems thrown up by Camus's description of the plague, the characters in *La Peste* remain . . . shadows. Yet it is not the spare style, maintained with marvellous consistency, which has brought about this reduction: it is the lack of perspective. The lives of his characters are without direction, without motivation, without development. . . .[2]

And Lukacs poses the issue, as he sees it, bluntly:

> The real dilemma of our age is not the opposition between capitalism and socialism, but the opposition between peace and war. The first duty of the bourgeois intellectual has become the rejection of an all-pervading fatalistic *angst*, implying a rescue operation for humanity rather than any breakthrough to Socialism. . . . It is the dilemma of the choice between an aesthetically appealing, but decadent modernism, and a fruitful critical realism. It is the choice between Franz Kafka and Thomas Mann.[3]

This is a formidable challenge to contemporary literary critics in the West, and not one that can be shrugged off with easy remarks about Stalin or Mao Tse-Tung. For if the dominant philosophy in the West today is 'humanism' or 'secular-humanism', we can

[1] Lukacs, op. cit., p. 51.
[2] Ibid., p. 59.
[3] Ibid., p. 92.

never for long forget that Marxism claims to be the most logical as well as the most hopeful form of humanism. This is not the place to discuss the claims of Marxism to be a total philosophy of life. At this stage in the argument all one can do is to suggest alternative views. First, there is the fact that the only two major talents to emerge from the communist world are Pasternak and Brecht; Pasternak, of course, is disowned by that world (though he belongs to it more closely than many anti-communists have liked to admit), and Brecht, as we shall see, is an ambiguous and perhaps ambivalent example. And second, that the phase of 'modernism' in the West, while open (I believe) to most of the criticisms Lukacs directs against it, has brought an honesty, a fearless 'looking at the worst' which has been gain rather than loss – we are all, even Lukacs, in debt to it. And finally, that there is in nature (including the nature of man) a resilience which in the long run has usually rescued it from final disaster.

Bertolt Brecht perhaps himself provides us with a good example of this last process. After his conversion to communism he tried to stay as close to orthodox Marxism as he could – and sometimes flawed his writing because of it. (Even Lukacs admits that Brecht is an unreliable witness for socialist realism in the drama.) And yet there are occasions when his instinct as a creative writer simply burst through his self-imposed fetters, without he himself being aware of it. I think of the problem of presenting his best-known play, *Mother Courage* (1938-9). When it was first played at Zürich, the critics were enthusiastic, especially about the central figure 'Mother Courage' herself, whom they described as a 'Niobe-like' figure taken from Greek tragic drama. Brecht was furious: he had wanted above all to avoid making her a sympathetic heroine. So he re-wrote the play before its Berlin performance, to bring out the communal aspect and make Mother Courage a more cragged, rascally character. This revised version was performed in East Germany, and the leading Marxist dramatic critic, Max Schroeder, who had not seen the first version, praised the play, and above all the character of Mother Courage herself, who appears 'a Niobe-like' figure taken from Greek tragic drama . . . ![1]

Another example of an artist's unconscious taking control of, and dominating his conscious purpose is one I cannot forbear to quote since it is charming and little-known. The French dramatist, Armand Salacrou, has in several of his published pieces described himself as a determinist. He even wrote one play, *Dieu le Savait*, to demonstrate a rigorous determinism. (It is one of his worst plays.) But he wrote another, which he called a 'Comedy-Ballet', to describe how a thorough determinism might be worked out in human life. Salacrou made his money in advertising: and this gave him an idea – is not advertising a form of thought- or wish-determinism? So, in this 'Comedy-Ballet' the hero,

[1] Martin Esslin, *Brecht, A Choice of Evils* (Eyre & Spottiswoode, 1959), pp. 203-4. (This is Martin Esslin's account: it is true that Esslin writes with a strong anti-communist bias, but his account of this episode is carefully documented.)

Poof, is a sandwich-board man. After initial failures to sell anything he suddenly discovers the secret, and becomes immensely successful. The secret is that 'to sell chocolates, you don't have to manufacture chocolates: you have to manufacture chocolate-consumers'. Soon he aims higher: he starts appealing to the 'highest in man'. The Papal Legate comes one day to thank him for what he has done for the Church: by broadcasts on the delights of Paradise he has pushed up the Easter communicants by 22 per cent. Though the Monsignor is disturbed that the pin-up girl whom Poof uses to advertise the Blessed Virgin (and who has produced numerous conversions) is not irreproachable in her private life. Poof replies triumphantly that she had herself been converted by contemplating her own photograph, and had just entered a convent. And Poof says he could teach God a thing or two:

> He doesn't seem to me to have had much of a flair for publicity. Look how inadequately he brought home the dangers of the Garden of Eden. I assure you, if I'd been in charge Adam wouldn't have eaten any other apples than those I'd suggested to him to eat. . . .

By the end of the play Poof is so powerful that a group of conspirators tries to oppose him: 'We must defeat him,' they say, 'if we want to remain human.' They decide to organize a vast 'anti-publicity' movement. Poof hears about this, and by now is bored with his own advertising agency. Since they have some difficulty in getting going, he offers his help – and by the end of the play he is launching a huge publicity campaign, entitled

'Down with Publicity'. In his earlier interview with the Papal Legate the latter asks Poof whether he isn't afraid of taking away people's intelligence by organizing their minds as he does?

Poof: Be serious. Do men need intelligence to live?
Monsignor: But you're making domestic animals of them.
Poof: Well, aren't cows happy in the meadow?
Monsignor: But – to substitute your desires for men's: that's a terrible responsibility to take on yourself.
Poof: God gave men free-will. He was a sly one – He hated responsibility. But I – I loyally accept the duties committed to me, and it's a heavy charge, I admit. Men no longer have any wishes but those I give them.

And the play ends with a conversation between Poof and a young couple. They are asking for happiness, and Poof promises to give it them.

Poof: What do men want? Happiness? All right. I'm going to launch 'Poof Happiness'. . . . I wonder God didn't think of it. After so much trouble in creating the world, there was so little left for Him to do, to give men the illusion of happiness on earth. . . . I can see, in my mind's eye, a lovely poster already: Soft colours; Dawn; a Sun-Rise . . . 'Be Happy!' And men will have nothing else then to do but breathe. It's the only thing I can't do for them.

The playlet is extremely funny – and that is the point. It seems to be a studied defence of determinism expressed in the powers of persuasion, hypnotism and advertising: but a satire like this could only have been written out of a profound (if unacknowledged) sense of the inviolability of man's integrity and freedom. And this peeps out of the text at one point, just before the end. When Poof has organized everything he can, has total power, and stands looking at the future, he is left after all a little sad.

Poof: Alas, alas. It's easier to be the Pope of men than the God of one's soul.[1]

In his discussion of 'modernism' Lukacs does not say very much about comedy. He might, indeed, have strengthened his case by showing the extent to which comedy has been replaced in the 'modernist' plays and novels by satire – a much thinner and more limited achievement. Nevertheless what I have called 'the resilience of the natural' asserts itself even here. Lukacs rightly (I believe) singles out Samuel Beckett as an extreme case of modernism – his novel, *Molloy*, for instance presents us

with an image of the utmost human degradation – an idiot's vegetative existence. Then, as help is imminent from a mysterious unspecified source, the rescuer himself sinks into idiocy.[2]

And yet Beckett's most famous work, *Waiting for Godot*, though it seems to present a totally unrelieved pessimism – it is well known that the author objected to productions of it which implied some hope – has had a universal appeal which belies its message. Why? Because, I believe, of the genuinely *comic* element of the two main characters, 'Gogo' and 'Didi'.

For what does comedy carry with it? I cannot put it

[1] Armand Salacrou, *Poof Comédie-Ballet* in *Théâtre* (Gallimard, 1947).
[2] Lukacs, p. 31.

better than in the words of Professor Nathan A. Scott, an American theologian and literary critic:

It is the function of comedy to enliven our sense of the human actuality, to put us in touch with the Whole Truth – particularly when, in the pursuit of some false and abstract image of ourselves, we have become embarrassed by the limitations of our creatureliness and undertaken to bring our life in history to an end by . . . some disillusioned flight into the realm of pure idea. Forsaking all the meretricious forms of eschatology, comedy moves toward the actual: it asks us to be content with our human limitations and possibilities and to accept our life in this world without the sentimentality either of smugness or of cynicism. And when we wish to be pure discarnate spirit or pure discarnate intellect, the comedian asks us to remember the objective, material conditions of life with which we must make our peace, if we are to retain our sanity and survive.[1]

For genuine comedy penetrates almost as deeply as tragedy itself into the realms where human decisions are fateful and even final and yet not ultimate. The close partnership of the tragic and the comic has seldom been more painfully and yet illuminatingly shown than in the terrifying novel, *The Blood of the Lamb*, by the American 'comic' writer, Peter de Vries. It is a novel about death – the death of a little girl. She dies slowly, and painfully, of leukaemia. Her father, the 'I' of the story, is a writer; he is, by the end, a widower, and Carol is his greatest image of, and hold upon, life. She is clever, pretty and enchanting. During one of her

[1] Nathan A. Scott, 'The Bias of Comedy and the Narrow Escape into Faith' in the forthcoming symposium, Nathan A. Scott (ed.), *The Climate of Faith in Modern Literature* (Seabury Press, 1964).

'intermissions' from hospital – when a new drug has temporarily stayed the disease – she goes to the movies with a boy-friend, Omar. She is turned eleven, he thirteen. They see a modern film, but, much better, extracts from some old comedies, with custard pies thrown around. They find the old better:

'And have you ever noticed, Daddy – Omar and I were just talking about it – have you ever noticed this,' said Carol, shaking off her coat, 'that after the one guy throws his pie and it's the other guy's turn, the first guy doesn't resist or make any effort to defend himself? *He just stands there and takes it.* He even waits for it, his face sort of ready? And when he gets it, he still waits a second before wiping it out of his eyes, doing it deliberately, kind of solemn, as though the whole thing is a – '

'Ritual,' said Omar. '. . . even the way the face is wiped off is stylized, as Carol says. First slowly the eyes are dug out with the tips of the fingers, then the fingers freed with a flip, then the rest of the face is wiped down strictly according to established rules.'

Months later, after several false rallies and relapses, Carol gets an infection, and dies in the ward. It had been a long battle between the disease and new drugs; but the disease won in the end. Her father had brought her a special iced cake for her birthday, which he had left in a nearby church when word had suddenly been brought that she was dying. Now, coming away from the hospital, he remembers the cake. He goes in to the church and retrieves it. Outside he notices the large-size figure of the crucifix, over the central doorway. His bitter and long mounting anger against the universe now explodes: and he hurls the cake at the Figure.

It was miracle enough that the pastry should reach its target at all, at that height from the sidewalk. The more so that it should land squarely, just beneath the crown of thorns. Then through scalded eyes I seemed to see the hands free themselves of the nails and move slowly toward the soiled face. Very slowly, very deliberately, with infinite patience, the icing was wiped from the eyes and flung away. I could see it fall in clumps to the porch steps. Then the cheeks were wiped down with the same sense of grave and gentle ritual, with all the kind sobriety of one whose voice could be heard saying, 'Suffer the little children to come unto me . . . for of such is the kingdom of heaven.'[1]

The juxtaposition of a 'Laurel and Hardy' film with the figure of Christ may seem a little startling; but in the context of this serious and moving novel, it justifies itself. However, if this illustration appears too directly theological for our purpose, we may instance another, this time taken not from a novel but from life. In his *Homage to Catalonia*, George Orwell once showed his basic compassion.

He was so kind-hearted that when he saw a Fascist soldier running along a trench and simultaneously trying to pull up his trousers, he [Orwell] was unable to bring himself to fire – a man trying to pull up his trousers is a fellow human being and not a Fascist, he argued.[2]

Thus in the comic is revealed the human.

[1] Peter de Vries, *The Blood of the Lamb* (Gollancz, 1962), pp. 191, 237.

[2] Richard Rees, *George Orwell, Fugitive from the Camp of Victory* (Secker, 1961), p. 11, note.

7

The Resilience of the Natural

›››◊‹‹‹

IN 1907 a non-Christian novelist, André Ruyters, wrote an anti-Christian novel which was sharply criticized by the Catholic poet, Paul Claudel. Ruyters wrote to Claudel expressing surprise at this: for he claimed to be an 'ally' of the Christians. Claudel wrote back:

> You say that we are allies, but that is not true. A Catholic has no allies, he can only have brethren. You claim to be the friend of order and authority, but you are a stranger to the sole source of legitimate command, outside which there is only caprice, childishness and tyranny.[1]

I hope that by this stage it will be clear that Claudel's statement represents almost the exact antithesis to the view taken in this book. It is now necessary, however, to try to review the evidence and to see what this view implies and how in detail it works out.

I. *The Gifts of Scientific Humanism*

We saw in chapter four that whereas nineteenth-century agnostics rejected Christian dogma but applauded Christian ethics, contemporary secularists reject much of the ethics and ignore the dogma.

[1] *Paul Claudel et André Gide: Correspondence*, 1899-1926, ed. R. Mallet (Gallimard, 1959), p. 271.

The great weakness of Christianity would seem to be that it had indicated neither a suitable outlet for the energies of aggressive extraverted individuals nor an adequate and positive goal for social and political endeavour; indeed, by its attitude of indifference to the larger social problems, it fostered the divorce between ethics and politics which many thinkers have in recent years deplored.[1]

And Professor Flügel, the author of this quotation, suggests that as a result of failing to provide the necessary outlets, Christianity has been regarded by men of action as representing nothing but a 'slave morality' – an interesting recurrence in the twentieth century of the reproach levelled against it by Roman civilization in the second and third. Christians will no doubt reply by pointing to the achievements of the Christian conscience in the history of Europe – hospitals, factory acts, abolition of slavery, homes for the old, for unmarried mothers, orphans, etc.; to the work of great Christian pioneers, St Camillus of the Red Cross, Elizabeth Fry, Dr Barnardo, and the rest. But the secular humanist will retort that most of these advances were made at the instigation of individuals, without encouragement from and sometimes with the disapproval of the organized Christian Church; that they were inspired by humanitarian feeling indistinguishable from that of non-Christian reformers; and that the public record of the Christian Church in social matters is in fact unimpressive compared with that of many other societies and taking into account the knowledge and resources available. A powerful case for

[1] J. C. Flügel, *Man, Morals and Society*, p. 334.

this has been made out by the Jewish humanist, E. E. Hirschmann, in his impressive book, *On Human Unity*.

A Chinese poet tells of a small pygmy people under the Imperial sway, from among whom slaves were regularly furnished for the amusement of the Son of Heaven. But a newly appointed governor neglected to send such slaves, and when the Emperor remonstrated, replied to this effect: 'I wish respectfully to point out that our classics say that each land must give tribute according to the nature of its products. Now this land does not produce pygmy slaves, but only pygmy people.' The Emperor then commanded that the tribute should cease, and from that time onward the name of the Governor was remembered with love among the little people in whose cause he had spoken.[1]

Mr Hirschmann says that he does not know whether this story has a historical basis, but it was told by a Chinese poet at the period that we in Europe call 'Middle Ages'. And Hirschmann contrasts a great Christian figure Sir (St) Thomas More, who attacks the evils of society

in a form that bears clear witness of how little he expected to be heard, how little he thought it possible to appeal directly to his fellows to join in strife against these evils. Christianity . . . considers itself a higher law than the Law of the Hebrews. But More can see and point out some fifteen centuries after its birth that in imposing the death sentences for offences against property, it falls short even of the Mosaic Law. It seems (or am I insufficiently informed?) that it does not occur to him even to urge directly and plainly to the leaders of the Church he upheld, not to speak of the civil

[1] E. E. Hirschmann, *On Human Unity* (Gollancz, 1961), pp. 64-6.

authorities, still less any broad public, that such evils should be condemned.[1]

Hirschmann has little difficulty in demolishing other claims, negative and positive, by Christians. He quotes, for instance, Mr Quintin Hogg arguing that 'the retreat from humanitarianism is causally connected with the decay of religious beliefs in our time'; but also as saying that 'All the great evils of our time have come from men who mocked and exploited human misery by pretending that good government, that is government according to their way of thinking, could afford Utopia.' But, replies Hirschmann, you can hardly say that, e.g., the First World War was made by 'Utopians' – it was made 'by the successors of the makers of the Holy Alliance, the Hohenzollerns, Habsburgs and the Romanoffs'.[2] Again, he refers to the great Encyclical of Pope Leo XIII, *Rerum Novarum*, often called 'The Workers' Charter'. This Encyclical defends property on the grounds that

man leaves 'as it were the impress of his individuality' on the soil he cultivates – therefore it should be his own. But private ownership of the soil is called right even when those who have worked on it all their lives and left 'the impress of their individuality' on it do *not* own it: whereas those who have left no 'impress' actually own it.[3]

And he suggests that the Roman Catholic Church never caught up with the Quaker secular humanitarians, etc., in condemning slavery. For surely the rational nature of man requires the freedom of his body, and that

[1] Hirschmann, op. cit., pp. 64-6.
[2] Ibid., pp. 172, 82.
[3] Ibid., p. 223.

bears the 'impress of his individuality' even more than the soil he might work on.

> So we're not surprised that this 'defence' of the working class (more than forty years after the *Communist Manifesto*) won no very deep response from members of this class.[1]

And Hirschmann concludes with making a claim that may seem today to have a rather old-fashioned ring, but which has to be taken seriously. It is that the concept of 'human brotherhood' *can* in itself furnish a real guide to human action.

> The belief in which Charles I died on the scaffold, that the majority of men have no business to participate in the government of the society in which they live, would be repudiated by both camps today. [Hirschmann is speaking of the two sides of the iron and bamboo curtains]. . . . The name of democracy, which each side now uses against the other, imputing falsehood to each other's claim, once gave at least some sense of common direction, and Marx could write in the name of the Workers' International to Abraham Lincoln, and he reply in warmth and sympathy.[2]

This claim has to be taken the more seriously since the collapse of 'the Socialist Sixth of the World' – I mean the disappearance of anything that can be called a monolithic world communism. The disillusion that followed upon Hungary (1956) is I think likely to be nothing compared with the disillusion following the (practical) break between Russia and China; and a body of people (I refer to the ex-Marxists of the *West*) that has lost its faith is in grave danger of intellectual and moral anarchy. The kind of Christian apologetics that flourished

[1] Hirschmann, op. cit., p. 223. [2] Ibid., p. 220.

in the 'thirties and 'forties, which not only predicted, but gloated over, the collapse of a Godless humanist world, always ran the danger, not only of a collective Christian *hubris*, but of a denial of God's providence. (I write as one who penitently has to admit to once having engaged in this kind of triumphal war-dance over the symbolic corpse of humanism.) The Christian, knowing that he is in a minority, should, on the contrary give every kind of support to even those movements which by their success seem to disprove the Christians' case. And this is even more important when we remember the place of the 'younger' nations today, of Africa and the East. The hopes for 'non-alignment' will depend, for their realization, upon the emergence of a genuine 'democratic humanism' (democratic being required to take a fairly wide and adaptable meaning) which cannot in the nature of things be either Christian, Islamic or Buddhist, though it will have to allow for these three, and others, as commitments within it. It is profoundly interesting in this connection to read the remarks of that distinguished African, President of the Republic of Senegal, Léopold Sédhar Senghor. He has described how in his days as a student in Paris, in the late 'twenties, most of his African companions were attracted to communism. But he, even back in those days, had a strong sense of his own African traditions. He was laughed at for it, regarded as a romantic 'primitive'; but he could not shake off the conviction that Marxism was something too 'Western' for Africa. Already he was developing the notion for which he has become famous since, the notion of '*négritude*', of the 'African Personality'. He admits that Africans like himself learned much from Marxism.

> The essential merit of Marx was not in having taught us political economy, as you might think, but *humanism*: he revealed to us Man in and beyond the economic history of concrete men, with their needs – material and spiritual – their alienations, their struggles, their future triumph in rediscovered liberty. . . . In this sense, Marx is the founder of sociology, that is, of modern humanism.
>
> The genius of Marx is not so much that he assigned man a notable place in the animal world (though he did this), for the great religions had done that before him; but he discovered and showed us in capitalism the process of *alienation* of this *free creative being*, man – even though this notion of alienation is of Christian origin.[1]

But there were elements in Marx that disturbed an African like himself:

> What troubled us about Marxism was, along with its atheism, a kind of scorn for spiritual values: this discursive reason pushed to its furthest limits, which turned into a cold materialism and a blind determinism. Disinterested by nature as African negroes are, we responded with the question: 'Why live at all if we are to lose both the zest and the reasons for living? And why act at all if the march of history is irreversible, if capitalism is condemned in the long run? And then, are we sure of recovering our *négritude* if we turn our back on it, of recovering its values if we simply take over those of Europe as they stand?'

And so M. Senghor was left, he says, without a clear way through the impasse: particularly the impasse left by

[1] Léopold Sédar Senghor, *Pierre Teilhard de Chardin et la Politique Africaine* (Ed. du Seuil, 1962), pp. 23, 24.

Marx's failure to solve the problem, how simply by building a communist society, *personalization* becomes possible in freedom? And where did he find his solution? In Teilhard de Chardin!

> He [Teilhard] replied to us with his notions of 'coherence' and 'fecundity'. Coherence in theory, fecundity in practice. These are, he said, the two criteria of truth.[1] And so, by helping us to make a clearing for the African Way of Socialism, he showed us how we could bring our contribution to the building of the *Civilization of the Universal* (as Teilhard called it): how to 'socialize' ourselves without denying any of the values of *négritude*.[2]

Senghor goes on to outline Teilhard's philosophy, and to bring out the way in which it allows for specific, individual difference within collaboration or coinherence. He refers significantly to Teilhard's stress upon scientific research, as almost a new 'mutation' of the human species:

> I must admit that Marx had not managed to rid us African élites of our distrust of the mere intellect. That's because too often he presented it as solely discursive, 'static and abstract'. But now we saw how happily Teilhard made it incarnate in the 'total Matter' and the very dimensions of space-time, in fact, placed it upon a wider and more concrete foundation. And so he made it not merely analytic, but intuitive, genuinely dialectical. That's how he made it into a power of prevision and technico-social invention at the service of *ultra-socialization*: a purposive power.[3]

Finally, Senghor admits that Teilhard hasn't answered

[1] Sénghor, quoting T. de Chardin, *La Vision du Passé* (Ed. du Seuil) III, p. 318. [2] Ibid., p. 33. [3] Ibid., p. 55.

all our questions: and he discusses two, the nature of art, and the diversity of religions.

How can a muslim or an animist react positively when he reads this Catholic author? I reply: just as the Protestants do, of whom a certain number of eminent minds are 'Teilhardists'. For the essential problem here is that of God. But at this level the question can be given a positive answer. The muslim God, like the animists' God, is in the last resort personal. He is the Centre and he is Love, upon which particular loves and particular centres converge.[1]

I have quoted Senghor at length, not because he is altogether representative – is there any African who could be? – but because this contribution of his (given to the Conference of the 'Association des Amis de P. Teilhard de Chardin', at Vézelay, 6-14 Sept., 1961) is not yet very well known in this country – it has not at the time of writing been translated into English. And because it is of considerable intrinsic interest. The reference to Teilhard's stress upon scientific research is important. For as we have seen in chapter one, the obvious and immediate appeal of the West to the 'under-privileged nations' has lain in its scientific and technological know-how. And this is sometimes sneered at: 'All they want is our gadgets'. To which the answer is, first, that you'd be only too glad to pick up a few gadgets to help increase food production if eighty per cent of your population were living below the poverty-line; and second that Western technology is more than 'gadgets' anyway. As Hirschmann says:

[1] Senghor, p. 62.

It is the discovery that discoveries can be made, rather than any particular theory or even any particular method, which lies at the root of the great revolution in our lives – one of the few irreversible changes in the history of man, which we associate with the name of science.[1]

Here lies, I think, the value of Mr John Wren Lewis' discussions of the nature of science in contemporary society. His contention is that, far from it being true (as so often said) that scientific materialism is corrupting the values of society,

> the most that science has ever done has been to expose a materialism already inherent in people's thought or way of living, and today the advance of science and technology is doing more than anything else could do to cure us of materialism, in all senses of that term.

This sounds a paradoxical claim, but he substantiates it thus. First, he says, if we take 'materialist' in its usual, pejorative sense as meaning predatory, manipulating, then religion (and especially in the Ages of Faith) was 'materialist' in this sense, as all magic is – magic meaning the use of unseen powers to impose our own will on others. But modern science, besides disproving the old-fashioned 'materialist' (in the other, philosophical sense) view of the universe, has found it necessary to introduce the 'personal' into the heart of scientific measurement itself. He quotes Sir George Thomson, in his Presidential Address to the British Association in 1961, that one of the great features of modern physics is that it has 'brought the observer firmly back into the picture'. Isn't

[1] Hirschmann, *On Human Unity*, p. 198.

that, comments Mr Wren Lewis, as far as one can go, from the 'materialist' side, towards bringing back the *person* into the picture? And further, he suggests that the very abundance which the 'materialism' of technology can bring will force us to ask the 'non-materialistic' question, what all this is for. And he believes that it is science that is responsible for 'de-Stalinization'.

Soviet Russia is an example of the fact that if you take over science, you take a viper into your bosom: there is something about science that disrupts ideologies. Hitler tried to subordinate science to racialism; the U.S.S.R. tried too, but soon realised (in its battle with Hitler) that science must have its head. The force which is in the ascendant in the world, the force of the revolutionary movement of science and technology, is one which breeds an atmosphere in which for sensitive people humanism goes without saying: it represents the growing consciousness of the human race about what the essential values of life are. For those who believe in God, it is something to thank God for.[1]

I must confess for my part that when Mr Wren Lewis goes on to make theological deductions from this analysis I do not think that he reaches a position which is consonant with the full Christian view of God. He speaks of 'the universal principle of humanity which is present in individual human relationships and which makes people in those relationships value each other's differences'; and goes on to say that 'then you are formulating a definition of what real Christianity means by God'. This is merely one man's view of what 'real Christianity'

[1] Mr Wren Lewis' position has been argued in various papers and lectures; I make these summaries (with his consent) largely from his Stephenson Lectures, Sheffield, 1962.

is, and is totally inadequate to express the most universal tradition of Christian belief. But we should be grateful for the light it throws on the human side of the analogies men must use to speak of God.

An interpretation of the growth of modern scientific thought which is not unlike that of Mr Wren Lewis, though I think far more profound and far nearer to Christian orthodoxy is that which was outlined nearly thirty years ago in the pages of *Mind* (and, alas, never republished – it seems to me an inexplicable lacuna) by the late Michael B. Foster. The three essays were entitled 'The Christian Doctrine of Creation and the Rise of Natural Science', 'Christian Theology and the Modern Science of Nature' and 'The Differences between Modern and Ancient Rationalism'[1]. They are too long, and often too technical even to summarize here (and they would require some modification today). But in general their theme is that 'Modern natural science could begin' (the author is speaking of the sixteenth century) 'only when the modern presuppositions about nature displaced the Greek: . . . but this displacement itself was possible only when the Christian conception of God had displaced the Pagan . . . Creative activity in God, material substance in nature, and empirical methods in natural science – all closely involved each other.' He shows that early modern philosophers, at the end of the Middle Ages, 'ascribed to nature the character

[1] Michael B. Foster, articles in *Mind* NS: XLIII, No. 172, Oct. 1934, pp. 446-68; XLIV, No. 176, Oct. 1935; and XLV, Nos. 177, 178, pp. 1-27.

which constituted it a possible object of modern natural science in advance of the actual establishment of that science'. For they held that a science of nature was possible: Descartes denied that final causes are operative in nature; and modern physics was based on the same view. Locke held that the real essence of natural objects is unknowable; the modern empirical sciences of nature presuppose the same. But, says Foster, these views are incompatible with the Aristotelian (and Scholastic) doctrine of nature, and the incompatible elements in the latter are similarly incompatible with modern science. So we have to ask: What is the source of the un-Greek elements imported into philosophy by post-Reformation philosophers which constitute the modernity of modern philosophy? And his answer is: the Christian revelation, and, especially, the Christian doctrine of Creation. This is worked out with a detailed care which cannot be reproduced here. But a few extracts may be given to show Foster's line of argument.

> The law which God imposes on the created world is not itself a product of God's will. It is not a command. It is the product of his understanding, and his will is wholly subject to it. . . . [Thus] the scientist is enabled by the use of his reason alone to enter into the reason of God, or, in Kepler's phrase, to 'think God's thoughts after him', and because God has made nature to conform to this thoughts, what the scientist discovers by this process will be in fact the laws of nature.

This sounds very dogmatic. But it is based on a careful analysis.

Two assumptions of modern scientific method are: 1. the scientist has to look nowhere beyond the world of material nature itself, to find the proper objects of his science; 2. (a corollary of 1.) the intelligible laws he discovers there admit of no exception.

Both are consequences of the doctrine that the material world is the work, not of a Demiurge but of an omnipotent Creator. It is because a Demiurge has to work in alien material that he never wholly realizes in it the idea which his reason conceives. The observer of a product of his, looking in it for the idea of the producer, never discovers more than an approximation. Whereas the divine Creator, not limited by recalcitrant material, can embody his idea in nature with the same perfection in which they are present to his intellect: and so the scientist can find in nature the intelligible objects he is searching for, not mere ectypes of them.

And this can be summarized:

1. This conception of nature as subject to intelligible laws which are fulfilled both perfectly in each case and without exception in any, is an indispensible presupposition of the mechanical science of nature peculiar to the modern world. 2. This conception of nature is implied in the doctrine that God is an omnipotent lawgiver, subject to no impediment whatever in the realisation in creation of the laws which his reason conceives.

It may seem, of course, to be merely a matter of historical interest that the rise of the natural sciences happened to have the accidental assistance of a theological revolution, and of little relevance today. The fact that, e.g., 'the Greeks, whether in their early polytheist, or in their later pantheist stage, did not attribute reality to sensible particulars', 'whereas the doctrine of Creation implies that the material is real *qua* material' – this may seem to have little to say to (e.g.) the place of technology in the twentieth century. But as Mill said long ago, the inductive natural sciences depend on the presupposition that nature is uniform – but the uniformity of nature cannot be established by the methods of inductive science. And Foster extends this: 'Every science of nature must depend upon presuppositions about nature which cannot be established by the methods of science itself.' If this is true, then the fact that a Christian attitude to nature lay behind (even if unacknowledged) the scientific revolution of more than three hundred years ago cannot be wholly irrelevant even today. (To 'sit down humbly before the facts' is much more appropriate to man's lowly conditions taught in the Bible than to believe that man has direct access to the workings of God's mind and can approach nature with certain abstract principles, i.e., deductively, in the manner of Aristotelian and Scholastic science.) And therefore the reverse may also be true: where there is a genuine understanding today of the nature and limits of scientific method, there can be discerned, however obscurely, a 'presence of Christ'.

II. *The Gifts of Criticism*

We have noted the positive contributions of scientific humanism, but does this mean that we can uncritically accept all that the modern world says – that somehow in all its findings, even though these are often mutually contradictory, there is, quite undifferentiated, the voice of God? And if this is absurd – as it must be – how do we differentiate?

The first answer may seem an inadequate one, but it was hinted at in the last chapter: by the language. On 28th February, 1962, a lecture was delivered in Cambridge which attracted a deal of attention. It was devoted to the works of Sir Charles P. Snow, and was given by Dr F. R. Leavis.[1] Dr Leavis said some extremely rude things about C. P. Snow's novels, his famous discussion of the 'Two Cultures', and his general ideas about the contemporary world. Unfortunately Dr Leavis did not pause to give much detailed substantiations to his very adverse judgements on these three elements: and as a result he gave the impression of arbitrary and oracular condemnation. And yet in fact none of the many who came indignantly to the defence of C. P. Snow were able to bring any evidence to show that Dr Leavis' literary judgements were faulty. And the bad temper which this Richmond Lecture generated (no doubt it was delivered in a bad temper too) had the effect of blinding most eyes to the real significance of the judgements Dr Leavis was making. Of Snow's novels he says that the author

> Can't do any of the things the power to do which makes a novelist. He tells you what you are to take him as doing, but he can give you no more than the telling. When the characters are supposed to fall in love you are told that they do, but he can't show it happening.

[1] F. R. Leavis, Richmond Lecture, 'The Significance of C. P. Snow', *Spectator*, 6th March, 1962.

And he complains that Snow's concern for the wider acceptance of science by those on the 'arts' side is based upon the mere ability of technology to deliver the goods ('more jam', as Snow called it) – and this conjures up

the vision of our imminent tomorrow in today's America: the energy, the triumphant technology, the productivity, the high standard of living and the life-impoverishment – the human emptiness; emptiness and boredom craving alcohol.

And Leavis concludes that the very rapidity with which change occurs means that we shall need all the more, not what Snow offers us (popular understanding of scientific method by literary men, popular courses in second-rate literary appreciation for scientists) – but mankind's

full intelligent possession of its full humanity (and 'possession' here means, not confident ownership of that which belongs to *us* – our property, but a basic living deference towards that to which, opening as it does into the unknown and itself unmeasurable, we known we belong). . . . What we need, and shall continue to need not less, is something with the livingness of the deepest vital instinct; an intelligence, a power – rooted, strong in experience, and supremely human – of creative response to the new challenges of time; something that is alien to either of Snow's cultures.

Basically Dr Leavis is right[1]: and he gives as an example of the view he is commending Tom Brangwen, in Lawrence's *The Rainbow*, watching by the fold in lambing-time under the night-sky: 'He knew he did not

[1] Nor does this judgement seem to me in need of any modification after the appearance of Sir Charles Snow's restatement: see *Times Lit. Sup.*, 25th Oct., 1963.

belong to himself.' If it can be shown (and I think that some of the extracts in the last section suggest that it could) that a modern scientific understanding of the world is in fact consonant with this essentially 'religious' view (Leavis stresses the adjective), then we shall be able to discern the 'presence' in it. But discernment means the kind of discrimination Leavis is urging upon us. And we must apply this to all claimants.

All claimants obviously includes specifically Christian claimants: and the scrutiny of the prose style of Christian publications is a task much more important than the resources devoted to it would convey. The fact that there has not been one literary critic of any distinction who has been found willing to defend the language of the New Testament section of the *New English Bible* is only an indication of something more important: that that language conveys the image of a middle-class, un-self-critical, middle-brow culture. Equally important is the task of scrutinizing the language of those scientific humanist works which we have been commending. I propose, therefore, as a sample, to subject Sir Julian Huxley's collection of essays, *The Humanist Frame*, to this kind of scrutiny.[1]

The volume was issued with a confidence and publicity which suggested that it would come to be regarded as a kind of *Essays and Reviews*, or *Lux Mundi*, of modern scientific humanism in the West. Its actual reception by the non-Christian public must have disappointed the authors: reviews in such journals as the *New Statesman*

[1] J. S. Huxley (ed.), *The Humanist Frame*.

and Nation or the *Guardian* were unfavourable, and seemed to imply that 'If this is humanism, we don't want it'. Some of the chapters were admirable as well as admirably written: e.g. Professor Waddington on 'The Human Animal', Professor Ginsberg on 'A Humanist View of Progress', E. H. Erikson's psychological study of 'The Roots of Virtue', Michael Tippett's sensitive 'Towards the Condition of Music', Michael Young on 'Sociology and Public Policy' and Harry Kelvin and H. Zeisel's excellent 'Law, Science and Humanism'. But there was little in these chapters that could not be welcomed by a Christian humanist (or, for that matter, by a forward-looking Buddhist or a devout Hindu member of Congress): and the language is mostly unpretentious and clear.

True, there are certain internal contradictions between the essayists, which are not merely a matter of style. Not only contradictions of detail: as when one contributor says that Japan shows that the problem of overpopulation can be overcome,[1] while another says that Japan is an example of the failure to control overpopulation![2] There is also a contradiction between the sort of conservative attitude represented by Kelvin and Zeisel's chapter on Law, which shows the law as a conservative force, and Mr Aldous Huxley's chapter on 'Human Potentialities' which seems to endorse the power of technology to manipulate human beings – and the language reflects the attitude. The lawyers seem in effect to reject Huxley's view:

[1] H. J. Muller, p. 409. [2] G. C. L. Bertram, p. 378.

What if our scientists could point out individuals who are very likely to commit a crime, although they have not yet committed one; is the law to act upon such counsel? Such thoughts come dangerously close to the aseptic visions of a 'brave new world'.[1]

But the most glaring contradiction between several of the essayists is in their pictures of the relation between the present and the future. Dr Muller, writing on 'The Human Future', says:

> To engage in optimistic reflections concerning our future while ignoring our present unparalleled crisis would have been a species of wishful thinking amounting to criminal negligence. But even as gunpowder, spreading the means of ready death, spelled the end of feudal separatisms and in time helped to lay low the overlords, so our present incomparably deadlier tools are bound, after a period which *in retrospect* will appear short, to usher in the planet-wide community of man.[2]

Professor Maurice Ginsberg however, with more informed modesty, says:

> The belief in progress is the belief that the quest for justice will continue. . . . There is no law of necessary or automatic progress. Men will not be moralized despite themselves, and knowledge alone will not suffice to moralize them. What is asserted is that morality is rooted in the rational nature of man and that historically there is a growing correlation between the development of knowledge and moral and social development. However, the correlation is incomplete and the future remains uncertain.[3]

But it is the sheer volume of empty rhetoric and the

[1] Kelvin and Zeisel, p. 340.
[2] H. J. Muller, p. 406.
[3] M. Ginsberg, p. 125.

excruciating badness of the style of so many of the contributors that makes one seriously wonder whether, if this is what humanity has evolved towards, evolution is as beneficial a thing as *The Humanist Frame* implies. Perhaps H. J. Blackham, in 'The Human Programme', is being deliberately bathetic and circular in the following, simply in order to make it sound epigrammatic – but if so it is a misguided attempt:

It is reasonable, then, to think that it is not beyond the wit of man to bring about situations everywhere in which it will be reasonable for men to behave reasonably.[1]

Oliver Reiser, in 'The Integration of Knowledge', writes at length, but on analysis three-quarters of it consists of tautology, tricked out by headings and diagrams which make it look precise and scientific.

Indeed, it is only a question of time before peoples everywhere, reduced to a common destiny by the coercions of science and technology (e.g., controlled thermonuclear power, automation in industry, the conquest of outer space), *and guided into co-operation through the overwhelming pressures of integrative psychosocial aspirations*, will accept the general ideology ('humanist frame') as the architectonic for an emerging planetary democracy. [Italics very much his.][2]

Dr Muller, the zoologist, is frank enough to admit at one point that

Unfortunately the great process of biological evolution . . . although so successful throughout the past three billion years in having automatically raised life-forms from microbes to men, can no longer be relied upon to carry us, by itself, still higher. For with the advent of modern civilization we

[1] H. J. Blackman, p. 141 [2] P. O. Reiser, p. 245.

are so effectively saving the lives and facilitating the reproduction of individuals, that there is ground for inferring the biological basis of man now to be actually deteriorating rather than improving. These mutations are of the most diverse kinds, expressed in physical, intellectual, moral or temperamental traits. . . . It is a serious question among geneticists whether this process, unless checked by planned counter-measures, may not ultimately, carried on over thousands of years, go so far as to result in the decay of civilization itself.[1]

However he soon brushes off this careful (though turgidly expressed) caveat, and returns to the optimistic, romantic froth out of which his scientific expertise sticks up like a jagged rock:

Science will . . . enter into the fabric of men's lives even more thoroughly than religion did in actuating the campaigns of the Moslems and Crusaders. However, quite unlike the fanaticisms of old, the lodestars of science, when rigorously followed, lead men to ultimate agreement and to common effort instead of to mutual destruction. At the same time, men gain through the use of science ever more effective means for peacefully attaining their ends; they have ever richer experiences opened to them, and a longer-range, brighter vision of what is yet to come. All this, suffusing into their appreciation of nature and of the works of man, into their art, and into their daily acts of living, will immeasurably enhance the whole of their culture. . . .

And so

Man will find one horizon after another coming into view on his triumphant marches of conquest over the interminable reaches of external nature and the similarly inexhaustible immensities lying concealed within his very own being.[1]

[1] H. J. Muller, pp. 408, 409.

On which the tempting comment, both as to style and content, is the soldiers' comment in war-time about the food rations in the mess:

> If we had any bacon, we could have bacon-and-eggs – if we had any eggs.

Examination of language is, of course, not an end in itself: it is a way towards assessing the value of the thoughts and concepts expressed in it. As Mr George Steiner says, there is no law of conservation of energy of language:

> There is evidence to show that reserves of feeling can be depleted, that particular kinds of intellectual and psychological awareness can go brittle or unreal. There is a hardening in the arteries of the spirit as in those of the flesh. It is at least plausible that the complex of Hellenic and Christian values which is mirrored in tragic drama, and which has tempered the life of the western mind over the past two thousand years, is now in sharp decline.[1]

The quest of his book is to find out why tragedy has died in the West, during the last two to three hundred years. And he finds the first symptoms of that death in the language.

> Our words seem tired and shopworn. . . . Set the counting-house prose of the modern historian next to that of Gibbon, Macaulay or Michelet. Where the modern scholar cites from a classic text, the quotation seems to burn a hole in his own drab page. . . . Languages only let themselves be buried when something inside them has, in fact, died.[2]

[1] G. Steiner, *The Death of Tragedy* (Faber, 1962), p. 313.
[2] Steiner, pp. 314-5.

Just as the possibility of writing great tragedy today seems to have faded, so the sense of evil seems to have largely disappeared from the English novel during this century.[1] Evil – not just moral 'right' or 'wrong'. It is almost a relief to read a novel from Germany, like Gunther Grass' *The Tin Drum*, in which some of the enormous vitality comes from the fact that the Catholic and Jewish background makes real blasphemy, and even a little magic, possible. With the disappearance of evil there has also gone a sense of genuine conflict. As I tried to show in chapter five, perhaps Freud alone among psychologists leaves room for this. And as a corollary of that, the note of judgement goes too. Mr Wren Lewis dismisses Mr T. S. Eliot's attempts, particularly in his verse plays *The Family Reunion* and *The Cocktail Party* (and even, less obviously, *The Confidential Clerk*), to convey the sense that reality 'lies somehow *behind* the things we know rather than in them'; and with that, dismisses the whole of 'magical' ways of thinking. But he does not seem aware of how much he is thereby throwing out – of how much he leaves us with – in the field of imaginative thinking. In the end he is leaving us with a scorched earth, on which no culture can grow.[2]

And, interestingly, Mr Wren Lewis' own instincts rebel against this. For his positive contribution is a

[1] Mr Angus Wilson pointed this out in four notable broadcasts; see *Listener*, 'Evil and the Novelist Today', Dec. 27, 1961; Jan. 3, 10, 17, 1962.

[2] J. Wren Lewis, 'The Decline of Magic in Art and Politics', *Critical Quarterly* II, No. 1, Spring 1960; quoted also in the 1962 Stephenson Lectures.

valuable, but essentially 'magical' view of human relationships. He shows this by quoting Freud's mythological phrase, 'Eternal Eros shall put forth new strength', as the hope for the future.[1] And I believe that the weakness of the secular humanists' *language* is related to their thin conception of Eros. We normally think of the distinctive features of man as threefold: language, tool and institution. But, as M. Paul Ricoeur has put it (in one of the profoundest essays on twentieth-century sexuality that I have read), the enigma of sex is that it cannot be reduced to these three. For 1. sexuality belongs to the pre-linguistic stage in man: and even when it makes use of language it shatters it (think of the lovers' babbling, their love-cries). 2. It belongs to the pre-technical stage in man: for even when man learns sexual 'techniques', the tools must be forgotten in actual use, for self-consciousness brings impotence – 'sexuality remains fundamentally foreign to the relation of "intention – tool – thing".' And 3. whatever may be said of the equilibrium of sexuality in marriage, Eros cannot be institutionalized. Its natural link cannot be analysed into 'duty', 'debt'. Its only law, which is not law, is 'the reciprocity of gift'. Hence the glaring failures of sexuality in the civilization that seems to know most about it and spend the most time studying it:

> Love, as our culture has fashioned it, advances between two chasms: that of wandering desire, and that of a hypocritical will to constancy – the rigorist caricature of fidelity. Happy – and rare – is the meeting in living fidelity between

[1] J. Wren Lewis, ibid., quoting Freud, *Civilization and its Discontents*.

Eros, impatient of all rule, and the institution which man cannot maintain without sacrifice.[1]

And this is surely why writing from outside Europe – from Africa, especially – is so exciting and invigorating. Not only because the language is fresh, mad, new-minted (like Mr Amos Tutuola's fantastic tales from West Africa, or Camera Laye's powerful imagination[2]). But because the age-old notion of sex and fertility as sacred (and demonic) has not been altogether lost there. (Read a novel like Mr Cyprien Ekwenzi's *Jagua Nana*, and you must be aware that even apparently indiscriminate sexuality there retains something of the temple prostitute's 'ministry' to the god.) Only the artist can express this. For as Mr Eliot himself once said,

> The artist, I believe, is more primitive, as well as more civilized, than his contemporaries; his experience is deeper than civilization, and he only uses the phenomena of civilization in expressing it.[3]

III. *That Which Abides*

The curious thing about the quotation with which

[1] Paul Ricoeur, in *Esprit*, special number on *La Sexualité*, Nov. 1960, pp. 1675-6.

[2] Or the vigorous poem *New York* ('for jazz orchestra: trumpet solo') by Léopold Sédar Senghor, pouring scorn on Western city civilization –

New York: I say to you: New York let black blood flow into your blood
That it may rub the rust from your steel joints, like an oil of life. . . .

(Printed in G. Moore and Ulli Beier, *Modern Poetry from Africa*, Penguin African Library, 1963, p. 51.)

[3] T. S. Eliot, review of Wyndham Lewis, *Tarr*, in *The Egoist*, Sept. 1913: cited in E. Drew, *T. S. Eliot, The Design of his Poetry* (Eyre & Spottiswoode, 1950), p. 55.

this chapter opens, in which Paul Claudel denies that the Christian can have allies, is that Claudel was from his conversion steeped in the Catholic tradition. Yet a notion that Christians can find common ground with non-Christians is part of the 'natural law' tradition which is so much a characteristic of Catholicism.

When Bonhoeffer foretold the advent of a 'religionless Christianity', and spoke of 'man come of age', and the rest, he perhaps little realized the storm of debate, of accusation and defence, of alarm and acclaim which would result. But among those who have all along believed in and taught a 'natural law' there need have been far less anxiety and fevered discussion: of course God does not leave himself without witness outside the arena of grace and salvation; of course there is a presence *extra ecclesiam*; of course St Paul's teaching in Romans about the law written in men's hearts is relevant to all that Bonhoeffer said.

This is easily recognizable as gross oversimplification. For one thing, the Catholic notion of the relation of grace to nature has undergone considerable change; the work especially of Père de Lubac on the 'natural desire for salvation', denying propositions which seemed to have been made by St Thomas Aquinas and taken as authoritative, is one example of this revision. The idea of a two-storied house of salvation – a ground floor of nature and a first story of grace – is no longer crudely held. Yet the traditional view of a revelation of God in and through the nature of the universe, and of man, is in a general sense still a mark of Catholic teaching. And the 'natural law' is one obvious aspect of this.

This notion of 'natural law' has been profoundly suspect, both in Protestantism and in the empirical tradition of the West. It has been dismissed as too vague to have any meaning at all.

> A basic philosophy of values must underlie any legal approach to the problem of excessive concentration of economic power, [says an American jurist, discussing Anti-trust laws in the U.S.A.] – but the answer to a problem which is as complex as modern industrial society . . . cannot be sought in dogmatic deductions from 'Natural Law' premises.[1]

And it has also been attacked as an essentially conservative principle – compare the remarks of Mr Hirschmann, on the papal encyclical *Rerum Novarum*, in section one above. And we could add that much American legislation is based on 'Natural Law' notions, propounded by Thomas Jefferson; and they were able to be interpreted for a long time as a defence of the sacred rights of property and even of racialism. A Judge of the Supreme Court in 1872 defended the conviction of a white man married to a coloured wife in Mississippi – where it was legal – but then living in Tennessee where it was not – on the grounds that the union was 'unnatural'.[2] The majority of legal philosophers and jurists in the West, over the past hundred years, have taken the view known as 'legal positivism' which rejects abstract notions such as Natural Law, and which in its extreme form is

[1] W. Friedmann, *Law in a Changing Society* (Stevens, 1959), p. 285.

[2] Case of *State v. Bell*, cited in John C. Wu, *Fountain of Justice* (Sheed & Ward, 1959).

expressed in the famous words of Oliver Wendell Holmes:

> The prophecies of what the courts will do in fact, and nothing more pretentious, are what I mean by law.[1]

Nevertheless there has been a striking change in this area during the past few years. The change is most clearly expressed in the important book, *The Concept of Law*, by Professor H. L. A. Hart, Professor of Jurisprudence in Oxford.[2] After a long discussion he concludes that there are 'five salient characteristics of human nature' which can provide the minimum content of a Natural Law. They are: Human vulnerability; Approximate equality; Limited altruism; Limited resources; and Limited understanding and strength of will. On this basis he constructs a modest doctrine of natural law which is not unlike that which lies behind the Declaration of Human Rights of the United Nations Organization. Hart also refers to the experience of a German jurist, Gustav Radbruch, who considerably modified, if not recanted, his previously-held 'legal positivism' after the Nazi tyranny, on the ground that a strict legal positivism made it impossible to make moral judgements on duly enacted laws. The Nazi laws were validly enacted, yet commanded behaviour which, according to one German Court of Last Resort, could be described as 'contrary to the sound conscience and sense of justice of

[1] O. W. Holmes, *Collected Legal Papers* (Harcourt, N.Y., 1920), p. 173: cited in H. L. A. Hart, *The Concept of Law* (O.U.P., 1961), p. 10.

[2] H. L. A. Hart, op. cit.

all decent human beings' (Oberlandesgericht Bamberg, 27th July, 1949).[1] And finally, a distinguished South African jurist, sometime Professor of Law at the University of Capetown, came to the same conclusion after his experience of the Nationalist Government's *apartheid* legislation during the past fifteen years. He quotes, as an example of legal positivism, Judge Learned Hand:

> I shall ask you to assume with me that the Constitution and the 'Bill of Rights' [*sc.* in the U.S.A.] neither proceed from, nor have any warrant, in the Divine Will, either as St Thomas or Jefferson believed; but on the contrary, that they are the altogether human expression of the state conventions that ratified them; that their authority depends upon the sanctions available to enforce them; and their meaning to be gathered from the words they contain, read in the historical setting in which they were uttered.[2]

Professor Cowan, after having seen the rigging of the South African Senate in order to push through racial legislation, etc., comments:

> With respect to Judge Learned Hand, if this view were sound . . . then I would ask you to consider by what possible argument you could deny to the people, at any time, the right to ignore the work of their predecessors, and disregard the constitution itself?

[1] 64. *Harvard Law Rev.*, 1951, 1005ff. And Hart in 71/1. *Harv. Law Rev.*, Feb. 1958, 593-629. There has been some dispute whether Hart correctly represented Radbruch's position; and it has been asserted (H. O. Pappe, 23. *Mod. Law Rev.*, 1960, 260-274) that Radbruch did not 'recant'; but though the matter is somewhat technical I am not wholly convinced by Pappe's argument.

[2] Learned Hand, Jr, *The Bill of Rights* (Harvard, 1958): cited in D. V. Cowan, *Liberty, Equality, Fraternity – Today* (Hoernlé Lecture, 1961; S.A. Inst. of Race Relations, Johannesburg).

And he finds the only possible answer in a natural law which

> postulates the existence of certain unchanging principles of law and justice which can be discovered by man's intelligence, but can never be nullified by his will. . . . Only by seeking to give effect to the eternal values, can there be any strength and hope. . . .
>
> That the doctrine of natural law raises difficult issues I do not deny; but men cannot expect to enjoy the decencies of social and political life unless at the same time they are prepared to pay the metaphysical and theological price which these decencies ultimately involve. . . . Those who attempt to assert the rule, 'Do unto others as you would have them do unto you', as a purely human convention, in fact denature it; and render it impotent against a more strident assertion of human will that might is right. Fortunately, however, in the world today, amidst all the welter and confusion, there is taking place a great revival of natural law study and thinking. This, I believe, is the most exciting and hopeful sign of our times.[1]

Problems in plenty remain. It would be absurd to think that the fears of Reformed Protestant theologians, for instance, could be allayed by language of this sort. A French Protestant jurist, M. Jacques Ellul, can go so far as to say that, according to the Bible,

> Man has no knowledge whatsoever of justice, as he has none of goodness. . . . Strictly speaking everything that natural man does is unjust. . . . There can be no study of law outside Jesus Christ. . . . This [biblical] understanding of justice radically destroys the idea of objective law and of eternal justice. Law comes into being only by the judgements of God, and these are pronounced according to the rights of

[1] Cowan, *Liberty*.

man. There is no secular law. Anything man builds up under the name of law is precisely non-law.[1]

The language is strangely close to that of Paul Claudel from which we started: I do not think that Claudel would have rejoiced in finding such an ally. And fortunately, M. Ellul later goes on to discuss law and civilization in a way that softens the edges, in practice, of his sharp dichotomies.

In any case, the argument of this book implies that the convergence of view among jurists, political thinkers, sociologists and scientists, towards a common understanding of what it is that makes man human, is, literally, providential. Whatever the ultimate inadequacies, from the Christian point of view, of this convergence, it is in itself theologically significant. The psychologist, Thomas Szasz, already quoted, sees the importance, psychologically speaking, of *hope* for man. This notion of hope, he says, has received new emphasis in psychology by those who 'see in man's need for hope a contemporary justification for religious faith'. He thinks himself that this need for hope does not justify 'from a scientific point of view at least, a retreat to irrationalism and an endorsement of religion for mental health'. But he grudgingly concedes that it might be valid for some people:

What should man be *hopeful about*? . . . Disregarding the broadly existential character of these questions, I wish to emphasise only that investing hope in religious faith is, psycho-economically speaking, one of the best investments

[1] Jacques Ellul, *The Theological Foundation of Law* (Engl. tr.; S.C.M. Press, 1961), pp. 40, 42, 49.

one can make. This is because by investing a small amount of hope in religion – especially in a Christian religion – one gets back a great deal of it. . . . [For religions do promise hope, and] few other enterprises, other than fanatical nationalisms, promise as much. . . . Hence, those with small capitals of hope may do best by investing their 'savings' in religion.[1]

However, for Christians to accept this would be to give way to the temptation of which Bonhoeffer so sternly warned us – of implying that God speaks to men chiefly in their weakness and sin. 'We should not speak ill of man in his worldliness,' he said, 'but confront him with God at his strongest point.'[2] In a searching paper, given to the Fellowship of St Alban and St Sergius in 1960, Professor H. A. Hodges tells of a man he knew some thirty years ago. He had grown up in a Protestant environment, surrounded by the preaching of sin and Atonement; but himself grew up without any sense of sin or personal relation to God.

It seemed to him in his early years that the approach to religion through the conception of sin, and of the Angry Judge, and of the Kind Father, was all too human and all too sentimental.

But he was tormented by a religious problem: the problem of 'transience, of finitude, of meaninglessness. In a world of change and relativity was there anything that was abidingly true or real?' So he welcomed the Buddhist teaching that there is nothing substantial,

[1] T. S. Szasz, *The Myth of Mental Illness*, p. 287, note.

[2] D. Bonhoeffer, *Letters and Papers from Prison* (S.C.M. Press, 1953): Fontana edition, 1959, p. 118.

permanent or enduring. 'The doctrine of no-soul appeared to him as a liberation from the selfishness and greed with which Christians . . . tried to cling on to their wretched little souls.' And he practised Buddhist techniques to strengthen this sense of transcience. Yet he still had a sense of what could be called 'The Great Invisible'.

> And when, at a certain stage, Christianity dawned upon him, it came through a sudden understanding of Christ, not as Saviour from sin, but as the Incarnation of the Great Invisible. . . . It was not until several years later that he underwent an experience involving conscious guilt and reconciliation, of a kind which any Methodist would recognise as an evangelical conversion. This was not at the beginning of his spiritual course, as the traditional evangelical teaching would lead one to expect; it only came when he was well launched upon it.[1]

Professor Hodges admits that this man was not typical of our age, for he started with at least this notion of the Great Invisible; whereas our age considers even this notion exploded. And he acknowledges that there has been a 'destruction of the visible faces of God'. But he believes that Christians must regard this as a 'purgation, a stripping, a breaking of idols in order that the true ikon may appear, a dark night of the intellect overtaking the Church'.

> And for the Church, as for the individual soul, the word on entering into the night is 'wait and pray'. That is after all the Church's work, to pray.

[1] H. A. Hodges, *Holiness, Righteousness, Perfection* (Fellowship of St Alban and St Sergius, 1961), pp. 9-10.

The Resilience of the Natural

For perhaps the hardest fact that Christians have to face is, not that secular humanists are increasingly agreed about the nature of a truly human existence, and about the goals for man; but that they seem to have discovered within man and within society a 'self-righting' factor which can deal with the crises in which that truly human existence is marred, or through which the road towards the goal is diverted or lost. Thirty-four years ago Mr T. S. Eliot prophesied that:

> The World is trying the experiment of attempting to form a civilized but non-Christian mentality. The experiment will fail; but we must be very patient in awaiting its collapse; meanwhile redeeming the time: so that the Faith may be preserved alive through the dark ages before us; to renew and rebuild civilization, and save the World from suicide.[1]

But what if the experiment succeeds? This is a tougher problem both for Reformed theology and for a Catholic theology of Natural Law, than the old problem of 'nature and grace', *pur sang*. The function of grace is to 'restore our wounded nature'. But what if it is found that 'nature is its own best healer'? What is to be the Christian judgement on that self-healing? Can we say that somehow grace is, improbably and invisibly, involved in the very process which seems to by-pass it? Or must we fall back on a more ultimate pessimism, and say that the healing is only apparent and only superficial?

This leads us to the margins of a theological problem:

[1] T. S. Eliot, 'Thoughts after Lambeth' (1931) in *Selected Essays* (Faber, 1932), p. 363; re Lambeth Conference, 1930.

and since this is not a theological book, I leave it to the professional theologians. I can here only suggest that we boldly accept that all Christian argument is circular[1] – but try to show that it is not viciously circular. Just as the being of God cannot be demonstrated to one who is not already in some sense aware of it; so 'man's ruined nature' – the effects of the 'Fall' upon human history – can only be persuasively argued among those who already have some concept of 'sin'. Yet these two concepts (God's existence, and human sin) have found their way into man's consciousness – and if we believe in God we must believe that he knows what that way is. For God cannot leave himself without witness to those, and even through those, who appear totally unaware of the true nature of their testimony. Humanists are fully awake to the fact that the era of economic affluence poses its own dangers: that 'I'm all right, Jack' is pride before a fall. If they can go a step further and see that pride as *hubris*, they will be close to acknowledging the Majesty which is implied in that very notion – for *hubris* is essentially insult, insult to the gods. And if they can thus see the dangers of economic affluence, they may be brought to see the deeper dangers of humanistic affluence – the terrible abyss that lies before a cosmic 'I'm all right, Jack'.

This is the sense in which those – like two recent

[1] I mean that in the end the Christian will always appeal to two texts, as his final defence before the unbeliever: Isaiah 51.12, 13, and John 19.11. I leave the curious to relate these texts to the argument.

Cambridge scholars, Canon J. S. Bezzant,[1] and Mr Howard E. Root[2] – who plead for a new 'natural theology' appropriate to our secular age, are, I'm sure, in the right. And it will be obvious from the last chapter that I should look in the same direction as Mr Root for such a theology –

> The best text-books for contemporary natural theologians are not the second-hand theological treatises but the living works of artists who are in touch with the springs of creative imagination.[2]

It is depressing to find one eminent theologian dismissing this plea off-hand – and still more depressing to find that when he thinks of 'Christian writers' the names that come naturally to him are those of the late Dorothy L. Sayers, Charles Williams and C. S. Lewis.[3]

I have entitled this chapter 'The Resilience of the Natural'. I believe that this phrase corresponds to a reality; and therefore that that reality is important for Christians to note and to appreciate. For if life comes from God, then wherever the living is found, even in the midst of death, there God must to that extent be active in it.

And so I find in the following (true) incident something of a parable of the divine infusing the natural with a vitality that is its own vindication. It is concerned with childhood, and therefore with innocence. And even the

[1] J. S. Bezzant in *Objections to Christian Belief* (Constable, 1963), ch. 4.

[2] H. E. Root, 'Beginning all over again' in A. R. Vidler (ed.), *Soundings* (C.U.P., 1962), p. 18.

[3] E. L. Mascall, *Up and Down in Adria*, p. 22f.

secular humanist who rejects the theology of sin and salvation acknowledges a kind of theology of innocence.

Some years ago two American psychologists, Wayne Dennis and his wife, of the University of Virginia, conducted an experiment (an intrepid, some will say a heartless one), which they described afterwards in their monograph, 'Infant Development under Conditions of Restricted Practise and Minimum Social Stimulation'.

The experiment was conducted with twin girls. (Were they the Dennises' own?) From the age of five weeks up till the age of fourteen months they were subjected to a specific kind of treatment, designed to find out how far infantile reactions are merely imitative, how far spontaneous.

For the first six months they were reared under rigid conditions. The babies were not allowed to see each other; they were

> handled with as complete unemotionality as the Dennises were capable of. . . . They did not speak before entering the room, did not speak to the twins, and did not speak to each other while feeding or caring for the twins. There was no demonstration of affection, petting, fondling, cuddling or smiling. There were no rewards or punishments, and a definite effort was made in the direction of indifference while handling the babies. Acts which would provide examples for imitation were avoided.

But, as the commentator on this episode (Dr Phyllis Greenacre, then Professor of Clinical Psychiatry, Cornell University) observes:

> The result of this emotionally sterilized environment is a little surprising, in that it was the experimenters rather

than the babies who broke down and could not maintain this unnatural status.

She summarizes the process. Since the babies had no one else to become attached to, their emotional responses 'became focussed on the experimenter to a provocative extent'. At seven weeks the babies followed the experimenters with their eyes. . . . At eight weeks their hunger-crying would stop when an adult appeared. Between thirteen and sixteen weeks, they began to show behaviour suggestive of the beginning of disappointment reactions. . . . During the fifth and sixth months the twins showed especially strong fright-like reactions to certain noises. But they smiled and laughed persistently when approached unless they were hungry. . . .

When in their eighth month, one of them seized the experimenter's hair and face as he bent over the crib, it seemed they had finally more or less captivated the experimenters, and they [the latter] began to set themselves free from the tepidness of their handling. For the experimenters began gradually to break down and talk and play with the twins a little every day. . . .[1]

We have the highest authority for believing that the resilience of the natural shown in this particular way and by these particular agents, represents a little kind of epiphany:

'*For of such is the Kingdom of Heaven*'.

[1] Phyllis Greenacre, 'Infant Reactions to Restraint' in Clyde Kluckhohn and H. A. Murray (eds.), *Personality in Nature, Society and Culture* (Cape, 1949), pp. 397-8; quoting account by Dennises in *Gen. Psych. Monographs* 23 (1941), pp. 143-89.

Select Bibliography

(*A complete bibliography may be garnered from the notes*)

Chapter 1

F. Boulard, *An Introduction to Religious Sociology* (Darton, Longman & Todd, 1960)

D. L. Munby, *The Idea of a Secular Society* (O.U.P., 1963)

D. T. Jenkins, *Equality and Excellence* (S.C.M. Press, 1961)

Chapter 2

Mary B. Hesse, *Science and the Human Imagination* (Philosophical Library, 1955)

Mary B. Hesse, *Forces and Fields* (Philosophical Library, 1962)

James Lambert, *Science and Sanctity* (Faith Press, 1962)

Chapter 3

W. H. Thorpe, *Biology and the Nature of Man* (O.U.P., 1962)

P. Winch, *The Idea of a Social Science* (Humanities Press, 1959)

A. O. Lovejoy, *The Great Chain of Being* (Harvard Univ. Press, 1936)

P. Laslett and W. Runciman, *Philosophy, Politics and Society, Second Series* (Barnes & Noble, 1963)

Chapter 4

C. H. Waddington, *The Ethical Animal* (Atheneum Publ., 1961)

Margaret Mead, *New Lives for Old* (W. Morrow & Co., 1956)

Select Bibliography

Chapter 5

P. Rieff, *Freud: The Mind of the Moralist* (Viking Press, 1959)

N. O. Brown, *Life Against Death* (Wesleyan Univ. Press, 1959)

J. MacMurray, *The Form of the Personal* (Harper & Row, 1957-61)

Chapter 6

George Steiner, *The Death of Tragedy* (Hill & Wang, 1963)

G. Lukacs, *The Meaning of Contemporary Realism* (Harper & Row, 1963)

Nathan A. Scott (ed.), *The Climate of Faith in Modern Literature* (Seabury Press, 1964)

Chapter 7

H. L. A. Hart, *The Concept of Law* (O.U.P., 1961)

J. C. Wu, *Fountain of Justice* (Sheed & Ward, 1955)

J. Ellul, *The Theological Foundation of Law* (Doubleday, 1960)

C. Kluckhohn and H. Murray (eds.), *Personality in Nature, Society and Culture* (Knopf, 1949)

General

Ninian Smart, *Philosophers and Religious Truth* (S.C.M. Press, 1964)

William G. Pollard, *Chance and Providence* (Scribner, 1958)

William G. Pollard, *Physicist and Christian* (Seabury Press, 1961)

Neville Moray, *Cybernetics: Machines with Intelligence* (Burns & Oates, 1963)

Hugo Maynell, *Sense, Nonsense and Christianity* (Sheed & Ward, 1964)

Index

Index